DAYBOOK

OF CRITICAL READING AND WRITING

daybook, *n.* a book in which the events of the day are recorded; specif. a journal or diary

THE AUTHORS
* Fran Claggett
* Louann Reid
* Ruth Vinz

Great Source Education Group
A division of Houghton Mifflin Company
Wilmington, Massachusetts

THE AUTHORS

❋ **Fran Claggett**, an educational consultant, writer, and teacher at Sonoma State University, taught high school and college English for more than thirty years. Her books include *Drawing Your Own Conclusions: Graphic Strategies for Reading, Writing, and Thinking* (1992) with Joan Brown, *A Measure of Success* (1996), and *Teaching Writing: Art, Craft, and Genre* (2005) with Joan Brown, Nancy Patterson, and Louann Reid.

❋ **Louann Reid** taught junior and senior high school English for nineteen years and currently teaches courses for future English teachers at Colorado State University. She has edited *English Journal* and is the author or editor of several books and articles, including *Learning the Landscape* and *Recasting the Text* (1996) with Fran Claggett and Ruth Vinz. She is a frequent consultant and workshop presenter nationally and internationally.

❋ **Ruth Vinz**, currently a professor of English education and Morse Chair in Teacher Education at Teachers College, Columbia University, taught in secondary schools for twenty-three years. She is author of numerous books and articles that focus on teaching and learning in the English classroom. Dr. Vinz is a frequent presenter at conferences as well as a consultant and co-teacher in schools throughout the country.

REVIEWERS

Susan Dinges
Mt. Olive Public School District
Budd Lake, NJ

Connie McGee
Pembroke Pines, FL

Elizabeth Rehberger
Huntington Beach, CA

Stephanie Saltikov-Izabal
Huntington Beach, CA

EDITORIAL: Barbara Levadi and Sue Paro
DESIGN AND PRODUCTION: AARTPACK, Inc.

Printed in the United States of America

International Standard Book Number 13: 978-0-669-53487-0

International Standard Book Number 10: 0-669-53487-0

1 2 3 4 5 6 7 8 9 10 - VH - 11 10 09 08 07 06

Contents

Building Your Repertoire

When you want to be good at something, you develop "know-how." If you want to be an expert hiker, you learn how to use a compass and read a trail map. You study cloud formations and other signs that help you predict the weather. You learn the color markers that represent a trail's difficulty. With more expertise, you look at animal tracks and know what animals you might encounter. You learn to distinguish the call of particular birds. Every time you hike, you develop new skills that make hiking more enjoyable and more interesting. Building a **repertoire** of skills and abilities is what it takes to develop your "know-how" as a hiker.

Using this *Daybook,* you will build your repertoire of **critical approaches to reading and writing.** You will develop know-how by practicing many techniques and learning how to use them strategically. As with hiking, you will learn techniques that are the "tools" for the development of your reading and writing skills.

INTERACTING WITH THE TEXT

When you interact with a text, you have a conversation with it. Imagine you are talking to a friend who hums and looks around the room as you try to engage her in a conversation. She probably doesn't hear a word you say. When you're reading, be careful not to do the same thing. You need to hold up your end of the "conversation" by paying close attention to what is going on. Keep your focus and "listen" to what the writer has to say. One way to stay active and focused is to *read with your pen*.

- Circle words you don't know or understand.
- Underline important phrases, repetition, or key images.
- Make notes near confusing parts.
- Ask questions.
- Make comments like: "I wonder..." "What if....." I don't agree...." "I like this." Use phrases that express how you emotionally react.

In the *Daybook,* use the **Response Notes** column to help you carry on a conversation with the text. As you read "Alabama Earth," notice how one reader interacted with the text. Add your responses to the ones already there.

Alabama Earth by Langston Hughes

Response Notes

Do I know him?

I think he was an African American educator.

Find out.

Shows Washington's importance

love this

nonviolent way to make changes

Huh?

(At Booker Washington's grave)
Deep in Alabama earth
His buried body lies—
But higher than the singing pines
And taller than the skies
And out of Alabama earth
To all the world there goes
The truth a simple heart has held
And the strength a strong hand knows,
While over Alabama earth
These words are gently spoken:
Serve—and hate will die unborn.
Love—and chains are broken.

PHOTO: BOOKER T. WASHINGTON

✳ As you read "Luck," another poem by Langston Hughes, read with your pen. Use your **Response Notes** to write questions or emotional reactions you have to the poem. Underline words or phrases that seem important to you.

Luck by Langston Hughes

Sometimes a crumb falls
From the tables of joy,
Sometimes a bone
Is flung.

To some people
Love is given,
To others
Only heaven. ✜

✳ Have a conversation about the poem with a partner or a small group. Compare your **Response Notes.** Discuss what you each think *luck* means to Langston Hughes. What in the poem leads you to think so?

✳ Imagine that you can continue your conversation with the poet. Think about what *luck* means to you and how you would describe the meaning in words. To get started:

- List a few words or phrases that describe what the word "luck" means to you.

- List objects, colors, animals, or other concrete details you associate with luck.

- How does your idea of luck compare to Hughes's idea of luck?

Hughes's description of luck	My description of luck
"tables of joy" luck is like love	

✳ Using your lists as a guide, write a poem to Hughes that portrays what you think *luck* means. You might want to write in the style of Hughes, starting one stanza with *Sometimes* and the other stanza with *To some people.*

Interact with the text by reacting to, questioning, or talking back to the author.

2 LESSON

Have you ever read something that seems like it was written just for you? If so, there is something in the piece that you were able to **connect** to your own experiences and feelings. For example, you might connect what you are reading to something else you read before. You might connect to an event about which you have seen or heard. When you take the time to make these connections, you gain a better understanding of what you are reading by comparing new information to what you know.

As you read "Aunt Sue's Stories," use your **Response Notes** to jot down any connections you make between the people, ideas, or experiences in the story and those from your own life.

Aunt Sue's Stories by Langston Hughes

Aunt Sue has a head full of stories.
Aunt Sue has a whole heart full of stories.
Summer nights on the front porch
Aunt Sue cuddles a brown-faced child to her bosom
And tells him stories.
Black slaves
Working in the hot sun,
And black slaves
Walking in the dewy night,
And black slaves
Singing sorrow songs on the banks of a mighty river
Mingle themselves softly
In the flow of old Aunt Sue's voice,
Mingle themselves softly
In the dark shadows that cross and recross
Aunt Sue's stories.
And the dark-faced child, listening,
Knows that Aunt Sue's stories are real stories.
He knows that Aunt Sue never got her stories
Out of any book at all,
But that they came
Right out of her own life.
The dark-faced child is quiet
Of a summer night
Listening to Aunt Sue's stories. ✤

Response Notes

like my grandfather

✳ Reread the poem and consult your **Response Notes** in order to complete the chart below. List as many connections as you can make to "Aunt Sue's Stories."

Connections to you	Connections to other texts (movies, books, etc.)	Connections to world events, places, or situations beyond your life
Sometimes I have a head full of stories to tell.	*Confessions of Nat Turner* created a vision of slavery and sorrow.	Current events in Africa demonstrate how people are still enslaved today.

✳ Share your list with a partner. What connections do you have in common? What different connections do you have? What, for each of you, is the strongest connection?

✳ Langston Hughes describes Aunt Sue as having a "head full of stories." You have stories, too. What story of yours do you think Aunt Sue would appreciate hearing? Connect to Aunt Sue, the storyteller, by telling a story of your own back to her.

Connecting your experiences and knowledge to the people and events in the story helps you better understand what you read.

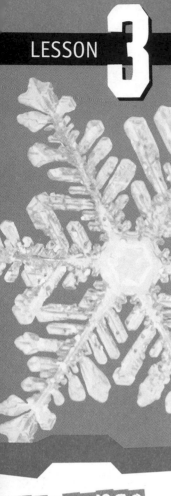

A perspective is a way of looking at something. You have certain perspectives because of your experiences. Your perspectives influence how you respond to what you read. Writers often share their perspectives. A writer's perspective is shaped by his or her experiences, education, and feelings. A poet who lives in Canada might have a different perspective on snow, for example, than a poet living in Arizona. The two poets' poems about snow would probably be entirely different—and shaped by their own experience (or inexperience) with winter.

Sometimes authors create characters with definite perspectives. Langston Hughes introduced a fictional character, Jesse B. Semple and a fictional "I" (not given a name) in a newspaper column he wrote for the *Chicago Defender*. This newspaper began in the 1940s and was owned by African Americans. Both Semple (nicknamed "Simple") and "I" have perspectives on the importance of knowing African American history. As you read, use your **Response Notes** to make notes about the differences in Simple's and "I's" perspectives.

Response Notes

from **The Return of Simple** by Langston Hughes

"Next week is Negro History Week," said Simple. "And how much Negro history do you know?"

"Why should I know *Negro* history?" I replied. "I am an American."

"But you are also a black man," said Simple, "and you did not come over on the *Mayflower*—at least, not the same *Mayflower* as the rest."

"What rest?" I asked.

"The rest who make up the most," said Simple, "then write the history books and leave us out, or else put in the books nothing but prize fighters and ballplayers. Some folks think Negro history begins and ends with Jackie Robinson."

"Not quite," I said.

"Not quite is right," said Simple. "Before Jackie there was Du Bois and before him there was Booker T. Washington, and before him was Frederick Douglass and before Douglass the original Freedom Walker, Harriet Tubman, who were a lady. Before her was them great Freedom Fighters who started rebellions in the South long before the Civil War. By name they was Gabriel and Nat Turner and Denmark Vesey."

"When, how, and where did you get all that information at once?" I asked.

"From my wife, Joyce," said Simple. "Joyce is a fiend for history. She belongs to the Association for the Study of Negro Life and History. Also Joyce went to school down South. There colored teachers teach children about *our* history. It is not like up North where almost no teachers teach children anything about themselves and who they is and where they come from out of our great black past which were Africa in the old days."

"The days of Ashanti and Benin and the great trade routes in the Middle Ages, the great cities and great kings."

"Amen!" said Simple. "It might have been long ago, but we had black kings. It is from one of them kings that I am descended."

"You?" I exclaimed. "How so? After five hundred years it hardly seems possible that you can trace your ancestry back to an African king."

"Oh, but I can," said Simple. "It is only just a matter of simple arithmetic. Suppose great old King Ashanti in his middle ages had one son. And that one son had two sons. And them two sons each had three sons—and so on down the line, each bigger set of sons having bigger sets of children themselves. Why, the way them sons of kings and kings' sons multiplied, after five hundred years, every black man in the U.S.A. must be the son of one of them African king's grandsons' sons—including me. A matter of simple arithmetic—I am descended from a king."

"It is a good thing to think, anyhow," I said.

"Furthermore, I am descended from the people who built the pyramids, created the alphabets, first wrote words on stones, and first added up two and two."

"Who said all those wise men were colored?"

"Joyce, my wife—and I never doubts her word. She has been going to the Schomburg Collection all week reading books which she cannot take out and carry home because they is too valuable to the Negro people, so must be read in the library. In some places in Harlem a rat might chaw one of them books which is so old and so valuable nobody could put it back in the library. My wife says the Schomburg in Harlem is one of the greatest places in the world to find out about Negro history. Joyce tried to drag me there one day, but I said I had rather get my history from her after she has got it from what she calls the archives. Friend, what is an archive?"

"A place of recorded records, books, files, the materials in which history is preserved."

"They got a million archives in the Schomburg library," said Simple.

"By no stretch of the imagination could there be that many."

"Yes there is," said Simple. "Every word in there is an archive to the Negro people, and to me. I want to know about my kings, my past, my Africa, my history years that make me proud. I want to go back to the days when I did not have to knock and bang and beg at doors for the chance to do things like I do now. I want to go back to the days of my blackness and greatness when I were in my own land and were king and I invented arithmetic."

"The way you can multiply kings and produce yourself as a least common denominator, maybe you did invent arithmetic," I said.

"Maybe I did," said Simple. ❖

✳ On the Venn diagram below, list details that reveal Simple's and "I's" perspectives on African American history. In the center, list any shared perspectives.

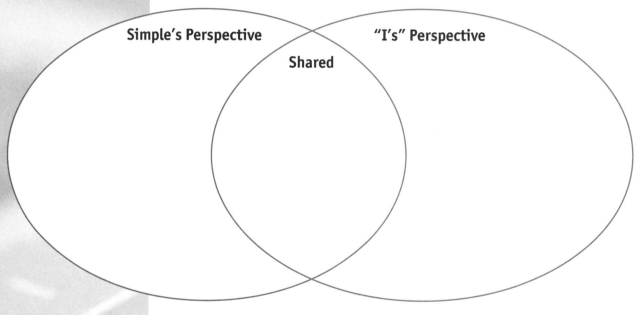

Simple's Perspective   **"I's" Perspective**

Shared

✳ Hughes creates two very different characters to share their perspectives on "knowing our history." Write a few sentences in which you explain what the conversation between Simple and "I" reveals about Hughes's perspective on people knowing about their own history. What details lead you to the conclusions you draw?

_____

_____

_____

_____

_____

_____

Exploring multiple perspectives helps you understand your own and others' perspectives on what you read.

What are the qualities of writing that make some writers more interesting than others to you? Certainly the subject matter makes a difference. When you have interests in science fiction, adventure, or horror, you naturally gravitate toward those. But the way a writer puts words together also affects a reader's interest. For example, what makes a piece of writing descriptive? Suspenseful? Fast paced? Good writers know how to use words to craft language that captures readers and draws them in. **Language and craft** involve a variety of elements that work together to create certain effects. Here are a few things we will look at in this lesson to focus on Hughes's use of language and craft:

- Choice of words
- Use of sound and rhythm
- Use of repetition

As you read "The Weary Blues," circle or highlight the language that makes the strongest impression on you. In your **Response Notes,** write what comes into your mind because of the language the author uses.

The Weary Blues by Langston Hughes

Droning a drowsy (syncopated) tune,
Rocking back and forth to a mellow croon,
I heard a Negro play.
Down on Lenox Avenue the other night
By the pale dull pallor of an old gas light
    He did a lazy sway. . . .
    He did a lazy sway. . . .
To the tune o' those Weary Blues.
With his ebony hands on each ivory key
He made that poor piano moan with melody.
    O Blues!
Swaying to and fro on his rickety stool
He played that sad raggy tune like a musical fool.
    Sweet Blues!
Coming from a black man's soul.
    O Blues!
In a deep song voice with a melancholy tone
I heard that Negro sing, that old piano moan—

Response Notes

describes rhythm?

interesting description

repeats, like in a song

© GREAT SOURCE. COPYING IS PROHIBITED.

"Ain't got nobody in all this world,
        Ain't got nobody but ma self.
        I's gwine to quit ma frownin'
        And put ma troubles on the shelf."

Thump, thump, thump, went his foot on the floor.
He played a few chords then he sang some more—
        "I got the Weary Blues
        And I can't be satisfied.
        Got the Weary Blues
        And can't be satisfied—
        I ain't happy no mo'
        And I wish that I had died." ✜

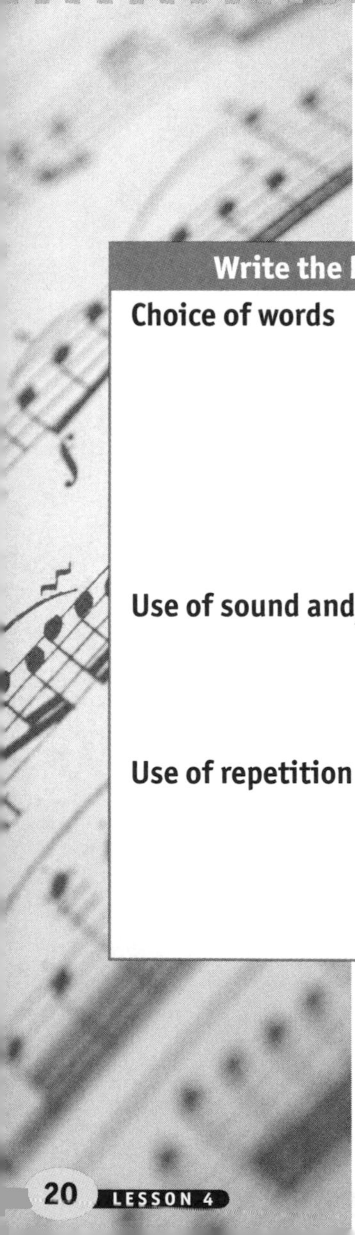

✳ What lines of the poem create the strongest impressions? In the Double Entry Chart below, write the line or lines from the poem in the left column. Explain your selections in the right column.

DOUBLE ENTRY CHART

Write the best examples of:	Explain why you think so
Choice of words	
Use of sound and/or rhythm	
Use of repetition	

✳ Share what you listed with a partner or a small group. After listening to what your classmates had to say, what words or phrases would you add to your chart?

✳ Hughes wrote about a piano player in "The Weary Blues." Think of a person about whom you would like to write a poem. You might choose to write about a friend, a family member, a famous singer, a movie star, or an athlete.

The subject of my poem is _____.

Spend some time thinking about this person in the following ways:

1 List several words or phrases that describe the person, both physically and emotionally.

2 Use a combination of sound and rhythm to describe the person.

3 Use repetition that will emphasize some particular good or bad quality about the person.

✳ Use your lists above and any other language that comes to mind to write a poem about the person.

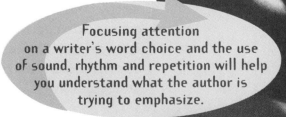

Focusing attention on a writer's word choice and the use of sound, rhythm and repetition will help you understand what the author is trying to emphasize.

STUDYING AN AUTHOR

Knowing about an author's life can help you better understand what you are reading. Not every story, poem, or article that a writer composes is autobiographical, of course, but most writers include aspects of their life experiences and memories in their writing. When you know something about a writer's experiences and concerns, you gain other important insights into the writer's craft.

As you read from Langston Hughes's autobiography, use your **Response Notes** to jot down any connections you make between his life and the poems and article you've read in this unit.

from I Wonder As I Wander by Langston Hughes

Response Notes

I came out of college in 1929, the year of the Stock Market crash and the beginning of the Great Depression. I had written my first novel, *Not Without Laughter,* as a student on the campus of Lincoln University. I had had a scholarship to college. After graduation a monthly sum from my patron enabled me to live comfortably in suburban New Jersey, an hour from Manhattan, revising my novel at leisure. Propelled by the backwash of the "Harlem Renaissance" of the early 'twenties, I had been drifting along pleasantly on the delightful rewards of my poems which seemed to please the fancy of kind-hearted New York ladies with money to help young writers. The magazines used very few stories with Negro themes, since Negro themes were considered exotic, in a class with Chinese or East Indian features. Editorial offices then never hired Negro writers to read manuscripts or employed them to work on their staffs. Almost all the young white writers I'd known in New York in the 'twenties had gotten good jobs with publishers or magazines as a result of their creative work. White friends of mine in Manhattan, whose first novels had received reviews nowhere nearly so good as my own, had been called to Hollywood, or were doing scripts for the radio. Poets whose poetry sold hardly at all had been offered jobs on smart New York magazines. But they were white. I was colored. So in Haiti I began to puzzle out how I, a *Negro,* could make a living in America from writing.

There was one other dilemma—how to make a living from *the kind of writing I wanted to do.* I did not want to write for the pulps, or turn out fake "true" stories to sell under anonymous names as Wallace Thurman did. I did not want to bat out slick non-Negro short stories in competition with a thousand other commercial writers trying to make *The Saturday Evening Post.* I wanted to write seriously and as well as I knew how about the Negro people, and make *that* kind of writing earn for me a living.

I thought, with the four hundred dollars my novel had given me, I had better go sit in the sun awhile and think, having just been through a tense and disheartening winter after a series of misunderstandings with the kind lady who had been my patron. She wanted me to be more African than Harlem— primitive in the simple, intuitive and noble sense of the word. I couldn't be, having grown up in Kansas City, Chicago and Cleveland. So that winter had left me ill in my soul. ❖

✳ Create a timeline of Hughes's life. List one key event of his life to the right of each number. In the boxes, explain the connections you find between his life events and his poetry and articles.

Born 1902

1.

2.

3.

4.

5.

Died 1967

✳ Langston Hughes won numerous awards for his writing. Imagine you are introducing him at an awards ceremony. Tell about Hughes's beginnings as a writer, the obstacles he overcame, and the messages that he conveys in his work. Why is he worthy of the award? Write your introduction on the lines below.

Studying an author's life and perspectives expands your understanding of the author's writing.

Interacting with the Text

Reading may be almost second nature to you. After all, you have probably been reading for many years. But what happens when you read about an unfamiliar subject or you read a new genre or type of writing? Readers strengthen their abilities by stretching their skills with new material. In this unit, you will practice **strategies** to help you read **nonfiction** literature about subjects that may be new to you.

This unit includes a biography, an autobiography, and a newspaper account of important people in United States history: a Native American leader, an American first lady, and teenagers who helped change our segregated society of the 1950s. By setting a purpose for reading and by visualizing what you read, you will make connections that will help you understand the information. You will also practice other strategies: questioning the text, building on background knowledge, and evaluating what you read.

SETTING A PURPOSE FOR READING

You should think about *why* you are reading something before you start to read it. Strategic readers know that their purposes for reading vary. How you read should change with your **purpose**. If you are reading for information, you might look for subheads or words in bold print that lead you to the information you are looking for. If you are reading for entertainment, you may want to enjoy every word or just read for the plot.

Before you read two excerpts from the **biography** *The Life and Death of Crazy Horse,* about a young Native American boy on a vision quest, ask yourself questions such as these:

- What do I already know about Crazy Horse?
- What do I know about Native American vision quests?
- What do I think I will get out of reading about Crazy Horse?
- Do I expect to be entertained or informed by my reading?

Use the answers to your questions to write one or two sentences that state your purpose for reading this selection.

_____

_____

_____

When he was young, the boy who became the famous Chief Crazy Horse was called Curly because of his unusually soft, curly hair. The first excerpt is a description of the boy and man who later came to be known as Crazy Horse. As you read, mark up the text. Use stars for surprising information, question marks for puzzling spots, check marks for ideas that confirm what you know.

from **The Life and Death of Crazy Horse**
by Russell Freedman

Response Notes

I would never have predicted this!

His own people knew him as "Our Strange One," and at times, he seemed very strange indeed. He wore no war paint, took no scalps, and refused to boast about his brave deeds. A quiet loner, he would walk through the village lost in thought or ride out on the plains to be by himself. His fellow Sioux loved to dance and sing, but [he] never joined a dance, not even the sun dance, and they say that nobody ever heard him sing.

When he was still a boy, grown-ups often discovered him standing in the shadows, listening to their conversation. When he grew up, he continued to listen. "He never spoke in council and attended very few," said his friend He Dog. "There was no special reason for this, it was just his nature. He was a very quiet man except when there was fighting."

Even his appearance set him apart. He was a small man for a fighter, with a wiry frame, soft brown hair, and pale skin. "Crazy Horse had a very light complexion, much lighter than the other Indians," Short Bull remembered. "His features were not like the rest of us. His face was not broad, and he had a sharp, high nose. He had black eyes that hardly ever looked straight at a man, but they didn't miss much that was going on all the same."

❋ What is your initial impression of Curly? Did you read anything that surprised you? Sketch or write your impressions here.

What you read next may change your impression. How could this intense, quiet boy do what he did? Continue to mark up the passage as you read.

One evening, when the Brulés stopped to make camp, Curly caught a glimpse of Conquering Bear as he was being carried into his tipi. Shaken by the sight of the dying chief, who looked so wasted and ghostly, the boy leaped on his pony and rode out on the prairie alone. He hobbled his horse beside a small lake, climbed a hill, stretched out on the ground, and gazed at the night sky.

He was about thirteen now, and he wanted to seek a vision. Sioux boys his age often went by themselves to some lonely place where they could commune with the sacred powers, hoping for a vision that would guide and inspire them

Response Notes

for the rest of their lives. Usually, a holy man helped a boy prepare for his vision quest. The youngster would fast, purify himself in a sweat lodge, and listen to the holy man's advice and instructions before finally setting out.

Curly had gone out impulsively, without the proper preparation, without telling anyone. Stripped to his breechcloth, he lay on the hilltop, staring at the stars. He had placed sharp stones between his toes and piles of pebbles under his back to keep from falling asleep. He would force himself to stay awake and fast until a vision came. He would try to enter the spirit world, the world that exists behind this one, where there is nothing but the spirits of all things.

For two days he remained on the hilltop without eating, fighting off sleep, his eyes like burning holes in his head, his mouth as dry as the sandhills around him. When he could barely keep his eyes open, he would get up and walk around and sing to himself. He grew weak and faint, but no vision came to him. Finally, on the third day, feeling unworthy of a vision, he started unsteadily down the hill to the lake where he had left his hobbled pony.

Discuss your reading with a partner. How well did you achieve your purpose for reading? How did having a purpose for reading help you stay involved in the text? Write notes from your conversation here and state your purpose for reading the next selection.

SUMMARY OF CONVERSATION WITH YOUR PARTNER

PURPOSE FOR READING THE NEXT SELECTION

Setting a purpose helps the reader stay focused and gain new knowledge from a text.

Strategic readers get more out of reading by doing what one student called "making movies in my mind." Some readers do this naturally. Others need to learn. Attention to descriptive details and having pencils or colored markers are key tools for **visualizing** and portraying what is happening in a text.

As you read about the vision quest of Curly, the boy who would later become Chief Crazy Horse, make movies in your mind. Picture what is happening and the images that Curly sees. Make sketches in the **Response Notes.** Mark words in the text that give you a vivid picture of what is happening. At the time of this excerpt, Curly has not yet received his "grown-up name." His father, a holy man, is the only one named Crazy Horse.

from **The Life and Death of Crazy Horse**
by Russell Freedman

Response Notes

His head was spinning, his stomach churning. The earth seemed to be shaking around him. He reached out to steady himself against a tree. Then—as he himself would later describe it—he saw his horse coming toward him from the lake, holding his head high, moving his legs freely. He was carrying a rider, a man with long brown hair hanging loosely below his waist. The horse kept changing colors. It seemed to be floating, floating above the ground, and the man sitting on the horse seemed to be floating, too.

The rider's face was unpainted. He had a hawk's feature in his hair and a small brown stone tied behind one ear. He spoke no sounds, but Curly heard him even so. Nothing he had ever seen with his eyes was as clear and bright as the vision that appeared to him now. And no words he had ever heard with his ears were like the words he seemed to be hearing.

The rider let him know that he must never wear a war bonnet. He must never paint his horse or tie up its tail before going into battle. Instead, he should sprinkle his horse with dust, then rub some dust over his own hair and body. And after a battle, he must never take anything for himself.

All the while the horse and rider kept moving toward him. They seemed to be surrounded by a shadowy enemy. Arrows and bullets were streaking toward the long-haired rider but fell away without touching him. Then a crowd of people, it seemed, clutching at his arms, trying to hold him back, but he rode right through them, shaking them off. A fierce storm came up, but the man kept riding. A few hail spots appeared on his body, and a little zigzag streak of lightning on his cheek. The storm faded. A small red-backed hawk flew screaming over the man's head. Still the people grabbed at him, making a great noise, pressing close around him, grabbing, grabbing. But he kept riding.

The vision faded. Curly felt someone kicking him hard. When he looked up, he saw his father. Crazy Horse had ridden out into the prairie to search for the boy. He was angry that Curly had run off alone without saying a word, distracting everyone from the dying Conquering Bear.

When Curly told his father that he had gone out to fast for a vision, Crazy Horse was furious. Seeking a vision without instruction! Without purifying himself! Without any preparation at all! Curly decided not to say anything else, not then. He would tell his father about his vision, but he would wait for the right time. ❖

※ This vision was very important to Curly later in his life. Because he trusted his sacred vision and followed the instructions in it, Crazy Horse was never injured by enemy bullets and arrows. Use a storyboard to help you see his vision. Don't worry about your artistic ability. Stick figures are fine.

1.

2.

3.

4.

Visualizing the events and details adds to the reader's understanding of nonfiction.

Asking questions about what you read is another way to learn. It helps you organize the new information in the text. But how do you decide what to ask before you read when you don't know anything about the subject? One way is to use a standard set of questions. When you are reading nonfiction, for example, you can create questions using the 5Ws and H that come from journalists: *who, what, when, where, why,* and *how. Who* is the subject of the article? *Where* does the action happen? And so on.

In an **autobiography,** the writer decides what facts to include. The writer may also reveal feelings, either directly or indirectly. Read the following excerpt from an autobiography by Eleanor Roosevelt (pictured right). As you read, circle the details that relate to *who, what, when, where, why,* and *how.* Be conscious, too, of what feelings she reveals about herself.

from **The Autobiography of Eleanor Roosevelt**
by Eleanor Roosevelt

Response Notes

In the beginning, because I felt, as only a young girl can feel it, all the pain of being an ugly duckling, I was not only timid, I was afraid. Afraid of almost everything, I think: of mice, of the dark, of imaginary dangers, of my own inadequacy. My chief objective, as a girl, was to do my duty. This had been drilled into me as far back as I could remember. Not my duty as I saw it, but my duty as laid down for me by other people. It never occurred to me to revolt. Anyhow, my one overwhelming need in those days was to be approved, to be loved, and I did whatever was required of me, hoping it would bring me nearer to the approval and love I so much wanted.

As a young woman, my sense of duty remained as strict and rigid as it had been when I was a girl, but it had changed its focus. My husband and my children became the center of my life and their needs were my new duty. I am afraid now that I approached this new obligation much as I had my childhood duties. I was still timid, still afraid of doing something wrong, of making mistakes, of not living up to the standards required by my mother-in-law, of failing to do what was expected of me.

As a result, I was so hidebound by duty that I became too critical, too much of a disciplinarian. I was so concerned with bringing up my children properly that I was not wise enough just to love them. Now, looking back, I think I would rather spoil a child a little and have more fun out of it. It was not until I reached middle age that I had the courage to develop interests of my own, outside of my duties to my family. In the beginning, it seems to me now, I had no goal beyond the interests themselves, in learning about people and conditions and the world outside our own United States. Almost at once I began to discover that interest leads to interest, knowledge leads to more knowledge, the capacity for understanding grows with the effort to understand.

From that time on, though I have had many problems, though I have known the grief and the loneliness that are the lot of most human beings, though I have had to make and still have to make endless adjustments, I have never been bored, never found the days long enough for the range of activities with which I wanted to fill them. And, having learned to stare down fear, I long ago reached the point where there is no living person whom I fear, and few challenges that I am not willing to face. ❖

✳ What are your first impressions of Eleanor Roosevelt after reading this excerpt? Explain.

_____

_____

_____

_____

✳ Imagine that you interviewed Mrs. Roosevelt for a publication for teenagers. Use the 5 Ws and H to write your questions. Follow your questions with what you think Mrs. Roosevelt's answers would be. When you write your interview, use the Question and Answer format, often known as Q and A, to help the reader identify who is speaking, as in this example:

Q: Mrs. Roosevelt, what was your main objective when you were a child?

A: To do my duty. This had been drilled into me as far back as I could remember.

_____

_____

_____

_____

_____

_____

_____

_____

_____

_____

_____

_____

_____

_____

_____

_____

_____

Using a standard set of questions is one way to organize information when reading about an unfamiliar subject.

USING BACKGROUND KNOWLEDGE

Did you know that you can learn something new by **connecting** it to something you already know? In fact, some people would say that that is the *only* way to learn something new. But how do you do that? When you read strategically, you think about what you know about the topic before you read. While you read, you compare what you are reading with what you know. By adding to and modifying what you know, you will build your knowledge.

You have probably learned about the U. S. civil rights movements of the 1950s and 1960s. But, in the newspaper column that follows, you may find some information that you did not know. Before you read, write in the box words and phrases for everything you can think of about the civil rights movements. Include names and places, too. You may create a web or a bulleted list.

✳ Write three sentences using some of your words and phrases. This will help you organize your thoughts before you read.

1 _____

_____

2 _____

_____

3 _____

_____

As you read, put check marks next to new information.

from "**Kids on the Bus: The Overlooked Role of Teenagers in the Civil-Rights Era**" by Jeffrey Zaslow

There's a true story we should tell our children about a bus, an African-American citizen and her yearning for equality in the segregated South of the 1950s.

No, Rosa Parks is not part of this story. This story is about Barbara Johns.

In 1951, Barbara was a 16-year-old student at a segregated school in Farmville, Va. About 450 black students were crowded into a school built for 200. Overflow classes were held in leaky, tar-paper shacks and on school buses, with kids shivering in the winter. Books and supplies were in tatters.

One day, Barbara missed the bus to school, and waited by the road, hoping someone would pick her up. A bus, filled with white children heading to their far-superior school, passed by. After it drove off, Barbara bravely decided to organize a walkout of her entire student body. Her leadership would help change America.

Our children are taught about Rosa Parks's refusal to give up her seat on a bus in 1955. They know about the Rev. Martin Luther King Jr. and his "I Have a Dream" speech. But many don't realize that the early civil-rights movement was often led by unsung teens. Some academics and activists now argue that by not sharing this hidden history, parents and teachers are missing crucial opportunities to energize and inspire today's kids, especially African-Americans.

"Rosa Parks, an older woman, is a wonderful symbol, but most black teenagers don't have a sense of the role played by people their own age," says Clayborne Carson, director of the Martin Luther King Jr. Research and Educational Institute at Stanford University. "When we speak about Rosa Parks, let's speak about these other people."

Barbara Johns led Moton High School students on a two-week strike. The NAACP offered to help their cause if they agreed to sue for an integrated school, not merely a school equal to the white one. The case was one of five reviewed by the U.S. Supreme Court when it declared segregation unconstitutional in the 1954 Brown v. Board of Education case. That year, Ms. Johns's family home was burned to ashes. She died from cancer in 1991.

"There were thousands of Barbara Johnses," says Doreen Loury, a professor of sociology and African-American studies at Arcadia University in Glenside, Pa. These were kids who made a stand to integrate lunch counters, community centers, sports leagues. As children in Columbus, Ohio, in the 1950s, Dr. Loury and her brother courageously entered a community pool and took a swim, even as white people got out and chanted, "We don't want you in our pool!" ❖

❋ Write two summary sentences that combine your new knowledge and your old knowledge. You could use a pattern such as "Although I knew _____, I didn't realize that _____."

1 _____

_____

2 _____

_____

Use your background knowledge to gain new understandings by connecting what you know to what you don't know.

The News
HIGH COURT BANS SEGREGATION IN PUBLIC SCHOOLS

Strategic readers make judgments about what they read. Anyone can say, "That's boring!" or "That's awesome!" But strategic readers go beyond such easy judgments. When reading nonfiction, they look for main ideas and evidence to support them. They question the authority and reliability of the evidence used. They also ask if there is another side of the story. Looking for information, asking questions about it, and thinking about it are all part of **evaluating** what you read.

Keep these considerations in mind as you continue reading about teenagers and their role in the civil rights movement. Mark places in the text that help you evaluate the key ideas.

from "Kids on the Bus: The Overlooked Role of Teenagers in the Civil-Rights Era" by Jeffrey Zaslow

One reason young activists have faded into history is because, early on, they didn't fit the image that civil-rights leaders wanted to project. Some were deemed too militant, rebellious or immature to be useful rallying symbols.

Claudette Colvin never became a household name. In Montgomery, Ala., nine months before Mrs. Parks took her stand, Ms. Colvin, then 15, refused to give up her seat on a bus and was arrested. Because she soon became pregnant, civil-rights leaders worried that her morals might be attacked, reflecting poorly on the movement if her case were taken to court. They preferred to showcase the 42-year-old Mrs. Parks, an upstanding citizen. Ms. Colvin, now 66, attended Mrs. Parks's funeral last week in Detroit, and was mentioned only briefly during the seven-hour memorial service.

In our sound-bite culture, we often simplify history into tidy stories: Dr. King was the black Moses who led his people to freedom. The saintly Mrs. Parks sat on that bus and became the mother of the civil-rights movement. ...

The lauding of superstars oversimplifies the real history. "The civil rights movement would have happened without Martin Luther King and Rosa Parks," says Dr. Carson, who is editor of Dr. King's papers. Because the movement was often "the story of teenage revolt," he adds, stories of young heroes would resonate with young people today.

As Dr. Loury sees it, learning about these brave young people can give children today "a moral and academic compass" that will guide and fortify them on issues far beyond civil rights.

But the old guard—institutions protecting the legacies of civil-rights icons—can be resistant to sharing glory.

Response Notes

Rosa Parks was not the 1st person to keep her seat on a bus.

The Rosa and Raymond Parks Institute for Self-Development in Detroit, a nonprofit education group founded by Mrs. Parks, chose not to get involved in a new traveling exhibit by the Smithsonian Institution called "381 Days." The exhibit focuses on the 381-day Montgomery Bus Boycott that followed Mrs. Parks's arrest.

While the exhibit shows that Mrs. Parks sparked the movement, it also recognizes the 50,000 people, young and old, who joined the boycott, walking miles to school and work, says a Smithsonian spokeswoman. At the Parks Institute, president emeritus Lila Cabbil says that the Smithsonian "wanted to feature other unsung heroes. We were concerned that [Mrs. Parks] wasn't featured prominently."

Actually, the Smithsonian is taking a worthy stand. The story of the bus boycott "has been recounted as a lone act of heroism," the exhibit's introduction explains. "But the truth is more powerful." ❖

✳ Write an evaluation of this newspaper article, which was written shortly after Rosa Parks died in 2005. Before writing, look back at the first part in Lesson 9. In your evaluation, (1) tell whether you think that this article presents another side of the story; (2) tell whether you think the story is accurate and believable; and, (3) explain your reasons, referring to the authority and reliability of the evidence and the treatment of all sides of the story.

_____

_____

_____

_____

_____

_____

_____

_____

_____

_____

Evaluate nonfiction by considering the accuracy and believability of the evidence. Ask if there are other sides of the story that should be presented.

Making Connections

Have you ever experienced one of those "aha" moments when you were reading a story? It's when you think to yourself, "Yes, I've felt that way, too!" Or, "Yes, I understand how this character feels." The "aha" moment usually results from **feeling connected** to the story because of similarities between the story and your own experiences.

Sometimes a story takes you into unfamiliar places. Your response then might be: "I've never thought about that before. This character teaches me something new." Or you might think, "This character makes me see a different world than I have seen before."

Sometimes a story can draw you in so that you feel as if you are living inside the story. When a story keeps you on the edge of your seat, makes you laugh or cry, or helps you to see things differently, it's because you've become emotionally involved. You are **connecting to the story.**

11

STEPPING INTO THE STORY

When you go to the movies, you ease yourself into a comfortable seat. You have snacks to enjoy. You wait for the lights to dim. Once the images flicker across the screen, you are in the story world.

Written stories work this way too. Writers hope you will care and understand when you read their stories. They also create a world for you to enter. Here are some ways to **step into a story:**

1 Ask yourself: What's going on? What's interesting about it?

2 Think about: What are my first impressions of the characters? Whom do I like? With whom do I sympathize?

3 Predict: What do I think might happen? What do I hope will happen?

Read the first part of "The Circuit," a short story based loosely on the author's life as the son of migrant farm workers. In your **Response Notes,** make notes about the three ways to step into a story.

Response Notes

The narrator seems friendly – he gets to know other workers.

from "The Circuit" by Francisco Jiménez

It was that time of year again. Ito, the strawberry sharecropper, did not smile. It was natural. The peak of the strawberry season was over and the last few days the workers, most of them *braceros,* were not picking as many boxes as they had during the months of June and July.

As the last days of August disappeared, so did the number of *braceros.* Sunday, only one—the best picker—came to work. I liked him. Sometimes we talked during our half-hour break. That is how I found out he was from Jalisco, the same state in Mexico my family was from. That Sunday was the last time I saw him.

When the sun had tired and sunk behind the mountains, Ito signaled us that it was time go home. *"Ya esora,"* he yelled in his broken Spanish. Those were the words I waited for twelve hours a day, every day, seven days a week, week after week. And the thought of not hearing them again saddened me.

As we drove home Papá did not say a word. With both hands on the wheel, he stared at the dirt road. My older brother, Roberto, was also silent. He leaned his head back and closed his eyes. Once in a while he cleared from his throat the dust that blew in from outside.

Yes, it was that time of year. When I opened the front door to the shack, I stopped. Everything we owned was neatly packed in cardboard boxes. Suddenly I felt even more the weight of hours, days, weeks, and months of work.

I sat down on a box. The thought of having to move to Fresno and knowing what was in store for me there brought tears to my eyes.

That night I could not sleep. I lay in bed thinking about how much I hated this move.

A little before five o'clock in the morning, Papá woke everyone up. A few minutes later, the yelling and screaming of my little brothers and sisters, for whom the move was a great adventure, broke the silence of dawn. Shortly, the barking of the dogs accompanied them. ❖

Complete the following chart to record how you are stepping into the story world. Use your Response Notes. Then share your finished chart with a partner.

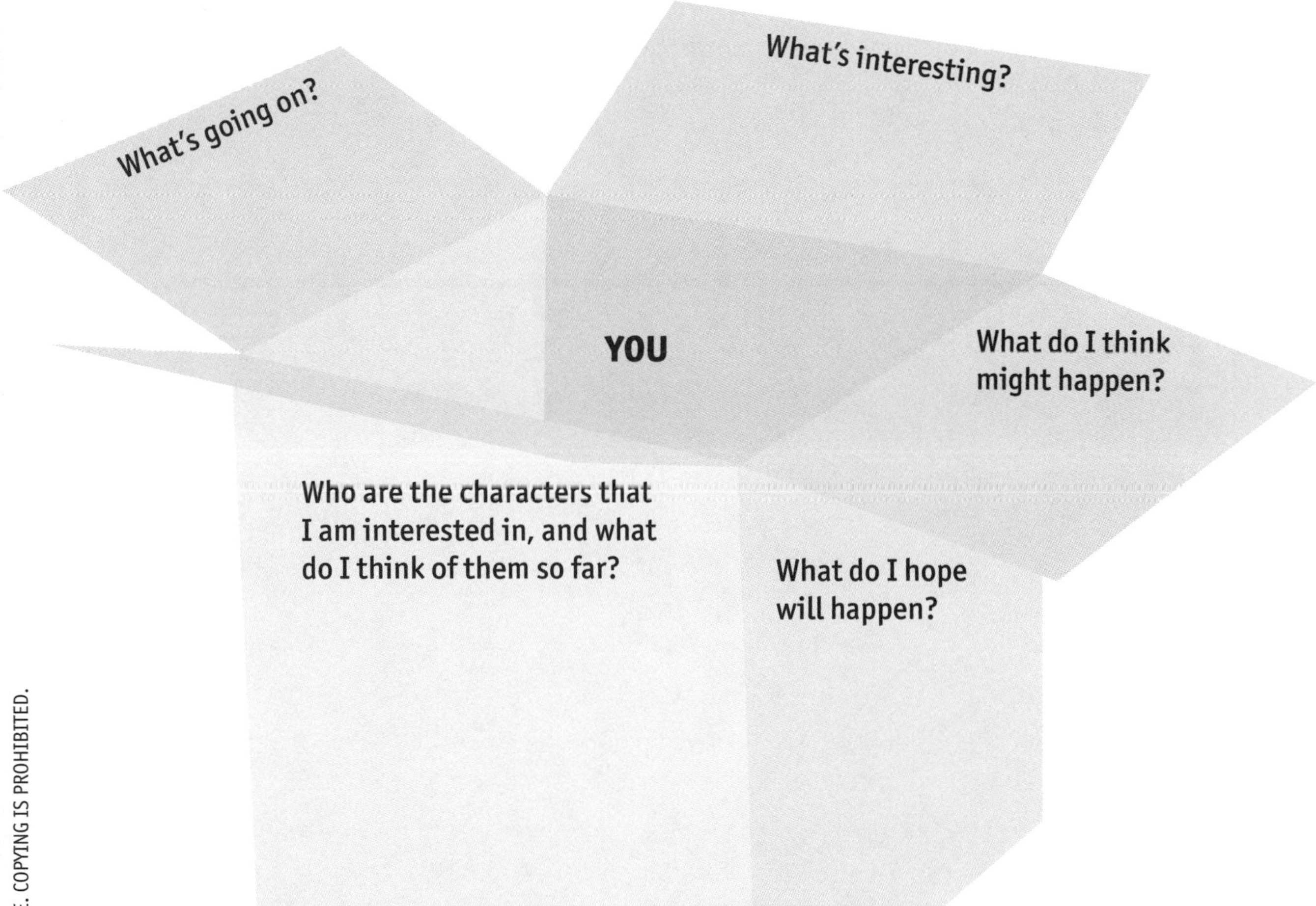

What's going on?

What's interesting?

YOU

What do I think might happen?

Who are the characters that I am interested in, and what do I think of them so far?

What do I hope will happen?

✳ Another way to step into the story world is to envision what is going on by creating pictures in your mind. In the following Story Frame, sketch two key scenes that you can visualize from the story so far. Give as much attention to detail as you can. Use colored pencils or markers if you wish.

Step into the story by imagining what is going on and visualizing the story world in your mind.

Just as at the movies, once you step into the story you start to "feel" it through your senses and your heart. If you do more than sit back and watch, you start to care about what happens. It's like that with a written story, too. As you get into the story, you start to care about the characters and what happens to them. You start to explore their situation and problems and "feel" for them. When you start reading a story in these ways, you **decide what matters.**

Continue reading "The Circuit." In your **Response Notes,** keep track of your emotional reactions. Record your responses and what you are feeling for the narrator and his family. Write down what matters to you.

from "**The Circuit**" by Francisco Jiménez

Response Notes

As we drove away, I felt a lump in my throat. I turned around and looked at our little shack for the last time.

At sunset we drove into a labor camp near Fresno. Since Papá did not speak English, Mamá asked the camp foreman if he needed any more workers. "We don't need no more," said the foreman, scratching his head. "Check with Sullivan down the road. Can't miss him. He lives in a big white house with a fence around it."

When we got there, Mamá walked up to the house. She went through a white gate, past a row of rose bushes, up the stairs to the front door. She rang the doorbell. The porch light went on and a tall husky man came out. They exchanged a few words. After the man went in, Mamá clasped her hands and hurried back to the car. "We have work! Mr. Sullivan said we can stay there the whole season," she said, gasping and pointing to an old garage near the stables.

The garage was worn out by the years. It had no windows. The walls, eaten by termites, strained to support the roof full of holes. The dirt floor, populated by earth worms, looked like a gray road map.

That night, by the light of a kerosene lamp, we unpacked and cleaned our new home. Roberto swept away the loose dirt, leaving the hard ground. Papá plugged the holes in the walls with old newspapers and tin can tops. Mamá fed my little brothers and sisters. Papá and Roberto then brought in the mattress and placed it on the far corner of the garage. "Mamá, you and the little ones sleep on the mattress. Robert, Panchito, and I will sleep outside under the trees," Papá said.

Early next morning Mr. Sullivan showed us where his crop was, and after breakfast, Papá, Roberto, and I headed for the vineyard to pick.

Around nine o'clock the temperature had risen to almost one hundred degrees. I was completely soaked in sweat and my mouth felt as if I had been chewing on a handkerchief. I walked over to the end of the row, picked up the jug of water we had brought, and began drinking, "Don't drink too much; you'll get sick," Roberto shouted. No sooner had he said that than I felt sick to my stomach. I dropped to my knees and let the jug roll off my hands. I remained motionless with my eyes glued to the hot sandy ground. All I could hear was the drone of insects. Slowly I began to recover. I poured water over my face and neck and watched the dirty water run down my arms to the ground.

I still felt a little dizzy when we took a break to eat lunch. It was past two o'clock and we sat underneath a large walnut tree that was on the side of the road. While we ate, Papá jotted down the number of boxes we had picked. Roberto drew designs on the ground with a stick. Suddenly I noticed Papá's face turn pale as he looked down the road. "Here comes the school bus," he whispered loudly in alarm. Instinctively, Roberto and I ran and hid in the vineyards. We did not want to get in trouble for not going to school. The neatly dressed boys about my age got off. They carried books under their arms. After they crossed the street, the bus drove away. Roberto and I came out from hiding and joined Papá. *"Tienen que tener cuidado,"* he warned us.

After lunch we went back to work. The sun kept beating down. The buzzing insects, the wet sweat, and the hot dry dust made the afternoon seem to last forever. Finally mountains around the valley reached out and swallowed the sun. Within an hour it was too dark to continue picking. The vines blanketed the grapes, making it difficult to see the bunches. *"Vámonos,"* said Papá, signaling to us that it was time to quit work. Papá then took out a pencil and began to figure out how much we had earned our first day. He wrote down numbers, crossed some out, wrote down some more. *"Quince,"* he murmured.

When we arrived home, we took a cold shower underneath a waterhose. We then sat down to eat dinner around some wooden crates that served as a table. Mamá had cooked a special meal for us. We had rice and tortillas with *carne con chile,* my favorite dish.

The next morning I could hardly move. My body ached all over. I felt little control over my arms and legs. This feeling went on every morning for days until my muscles finally got used to the work.

It was Monday, the first week of November. The grape season was over and I could now go to school. I woke up early that morning and lay in bed, looking at the stars and savoring the thought of not going to work and of starting sixth grade for the first time that year. Since I could not sleep, I decided to get up and join Papá and Roberto at breakfast. I sat at the table across from Roberto, but I kept my head down. I did not want to look up and face him. I knew he was sad. He was not going to school today. He was not going tomorrow, or next week, or next month. He would not go until the cotton season was over, and that was sometime in February. I rubbed my hands together and watched the dry, acid stained skin fall to the floor in little rolls.

When Papá and Roberto left for work, I felt relief. I walked to the top of a small grade next to the shack and watched the *Carcanchita* disappear in the distance in a cloud of dust.

Two hours later, around eight o'clock, I stood by the side of the road waiting for school bus number twenty. When it arrived I climbed in. Everyone was busy either talking or yelling. I sat in an empty seat in the back. ❖

✳ Stories talk to us. What are the four most important things this part of the story says to you? List them in order of importance, starting with the most important.

1 _____

_____

2 _____

_____

3 _____

_____

4 _____

_____

✳ Describe your feelings about the family and their situation. What aspects of their situation matter to you? When you finish writing, share what you wrote with a partner or a small group.

_____

_____

_____

_____

_____

_____

_____

_____

Connect to the story by deciding what's important to you as you learn what the characters are feeling and experiencing.

INFERRING MEANING THROUGH THE STORY

A story sometimes has meaning beyond the literal meaning of the words and the action of the story. The story may imply, or suggest, other interpretations of the words or actions. Ask yourself: What ideas and meaning does this story explore? What does this story teach you about migrant farm workers and the life they live?

Read the last part of "The Circuit." In your **Response Notes,** keep track of what you are learning from the story and your thoughts and feelings about it.

from "**The Circuit**" by Francisco Jiménez

Response Notes

I wonder how many schools the author went to.

When the bus stopped in front of the school, I felt very nervous. I looked out the bus window and saw boys and girls carrying books under their arms. I put my hands in my pants pocket and walked to the principal's office. When I entered I heard a woman's voice say: "May I help you?" I was startled. I had not heard English for months. For a few seconds I remained speechless. I looked at the lady who waited for an answer. My first instinct was to answer her in Spanish, but I held back. Finally, after struggling for English words, I managed to tell her that I wanted to enroll in the sixth grade. After answering many questions, I was led to the classroom.

Mr. Lema, the sixth grade teacher, greeted me and assigned me a desk. He then introduced me to the class. I was so nervous and scared at that moment when everyone's eyes were on me that I wished I were with Papá and Roberto picking cotton. After taking roll, Mr. Lema gave the class the assignment for the first hour. "The first thing we have to do this morning is finish reading the story we began yesterday," he said enthusiastically. He walked up to me, handed me an English book, and asked me to read. "We are on page 125," he said politely. When I heard this, I felt my blood rush to my head; I felt dizzy. "Would you like to read?" he asked hesitantly. I opened the book to page 125. My mouth was dry. My eyes began to water. I could not begin, "You can read later," Mr. Lema said understandingly.

For the rest of the reading period I kept getting angrier and angrier with myself. I should have read, I thought to myself.

During recess I went into the restroom and opened my English book to page 125. I began to read in a low voice, pretending I was in class. There were many words I did not know. I closed the book and headed back to the classroom.

Mr. Lema was sitting at his desk correcting papers. When I entered he looked up at me and smiled. I felt better. I walked up to him and asked if he could help me with the new words. "Gladly," he said.

The rest of the month I spent my lunch hours working on English with Mr. Lema, my best friend at school.

One Friday during lunch hour Mr. Lema asked me to take a walk with him to the music room. "Do you like music?" he asked me as we entered the building.

"Yes, I like *corridos*," I answered. He then picked up a trumpet, blew on it and handed it to me. The sound gave me goose bumps. I knew that sound. I had heard it in many *corridos.* "How would you like to learn how to play it?" he asked. He must have read my face because before I could answer, he added: "I'll teach you how to play it during our lunch hours."

That day I could hardly wait to get home to tell Papá and Mamá the great news. As I got off the bus, my little brothers and sisters ran up to meet me. They were yelling and screaming. I thought they were happy to see me, but when I opened the door to our shack, I saw that everything we owned was neatly packed in cardboard boxes. ✢

* Review what you've written in your **Response Notes.** Do a quick write to explore what you think are the big issues and ideas behind the story.

_____

_____

_____

_____

_____

_____

* Turn to a partner and share what each of you has written. Compare your impressions of the ideas and messages behind the story.

When you look at the meaning *behind* the story, you figure out what particular words, actions, or gestures mean. For example, if you turned to a classmate right now and said: "I wouldn't want to live on the circuit," that person would probably understand your reference to the title of the story you just read. Your classmate **infers** meaning beyond the word *circuit*. **Inferences** are the small understandings that you make while you read. Inferences become the meaning behind the story.

※ In the following chart, write your best understanding of what the following story elements mean and why you think so.

INFERENCE CHART

From the story	What it means	Why I think so
"As we drove away, I felt a lump in my throat." (p. 43)		
"Here comes the school bus," he whispered loudly in alarm. (p. 44)		
Neatly packed cardboard boxes (p. 47)		
The narrator isn't named.		
Title "The Circuit"		
Choose a sentence or an idea.		
Choose a sentence or an idea.		

Make inferences about the meaning behind the story in order to better understand what it has to say about life and human experiences.

Another way a reader can **connect** to a story is by researching information about the issues raised. For example, in "The Circuit" the family lives in difficult conditions. They find it necessary to move frequently. What are the conditions that make this necessary? Read the following excerpt from a newspaper article that examines migrant farm workers' issues. In your **Response Notes,** record connections you make to the story and your reactions to the information provided.

from "In the Strawberry Fields" by Eric Schlosser

Response Notes

The San Andreas labor camp is a small slum set amid rolling hills and strawberry fields not far from Watsonville. For most of the year this bleak collection of gray wooden barracks has about 350 residents, mainly strawberry workers and their families, but at the peak of the harvest hundreds more cram into its forty apartments. Last summer there was a major outbreak of tuberculosis at the camp, fueled by crowded living quarters and poor building design. The bedrooms occupy a central corridor of the barracks; none has a window. A superior-court judge recently held the landlord responsible for maintaining "a public nuisance" and for violating local fire, health, safety, building, and zoning codes. Nevertheless, the tenants continue to pay 500 a month for their two-bedroom apartments and feel lucky to have a roof over their heads. As I walked around the camp, there were children everywhere, running and playing in the dirt courtyards, oblivious of the squalor.

It was mid-April, and heavy rains the previous month had flooded hundreds of acres, scattering bright-blue plastic barrels from the nearby Smuckers plant across local strawberry fields and embedding them in the mud. Many fields that had not been flooded had still been damaged by the rains. The sky was overcast, more bad weather was coming, and a year's income for these workers would be determined in the next few months. Half a dozen strawberry pickers, leaning against parked cars, told me that at this point in the season they usually worked in the fields eight or ten hours a day. Only one of them was employed at the moment. Each morning the others visited the strawberry farm on a nearby hillside, inquired about work, and were turned away. The foreman, who had hired them for years, said to try again next week.

Harvest work in the strawberry fields, like most seasonal farm work in California, is considered "at will." There is no contract, no seniority, no obligation beyond the day-to-day. A grower hires and fires workers as necessary, without need for explanation. It makes no difference whether the migrant has been an employee for six days or six years. The terms of employment are laid down on a daily basis. If the grower wants slow and careful work, wages are paid by the hour. If the grower wants berries quickly removed from the field, the wages are piece-rate, providing an incentive to move fast. A migrant often does not know how long the workday will last or what the wage rate will be until he or she arrives at the field that morning. There might be two weeks of ten-hour days followed by a week of no work at all, depending on the weather and the market. ❖

✳ Both the story and the article you just read give you information about the difficult circumstances that migrant farm workers face. Lack of adequate housing, for example, is a problem. Select three key problems and record them on the chart. Use details from both the story and the article.

Problem:
Details:
Problem:
Details:
Problem:
Details:

✳ Select one of the migrant worker problems. Explain why it is an important problem and how the problem might be solved.

1 The issue: _____

_____

2 Why it is an important problem: _____

_____

3 Possible solutions: _____

_____

_____

_____

_____

Connect what you read to the larger issues in the world by researching the issues and sharing your understanding of them with others.

15 LESSON

Here's an example of a high school student's response to learning about the migrant farm workers' situation. Gloria Verastegui read about Cesar Chavez (photo right), a man who took action to organize the grape pickers in California so they would have better wages and working conditions. While his efforts were not entirely successful, he did help bring attention to the issues.

from "**A Street Name That Hits Home**" by Tara Malone

Response Notes

His was a name relegated to history books, where she read of his efforts to shield migrant workers from awful work conditions and miserly pay. But it wasn't until the Elgin High School junior recently launched a campaign to give Maroon Drive outside her school the honorary name of Cesar Chavez Drive that Verastegui learned how many Elgin residents Chavez affected with his grape boycotts, hunger fasts and community organizing.

Her dad included. A former potato picker, Verastegui's father ditched school for the fields, where he worked all day and much of the night to help his family in Mexico. Also among them was James Logan, the Elgin High dean's assistant who gave up grapes and wine in the early 1970s when Chavez called for a boycott demanding farm workers' right to organize and bargain collectively.

Chavez founded and led for 31 years the United Farm Workers of America. He died in 1993.

"His legacy is still going on," Verastegui said Monday. "There's a lot of people around Elgin who worked with him or who felt his work in their lives." To celebrate Chavez's efforts, which warranted the 1994 Presidential Medal of Freedom, Verastegui and four other Elgin High students hatched a plan to give a second, honorary name to the road in front of their school. They will unveil the proposal to Elgin High administrators, Elgin City Council members and Lt. Gov. Pat Quinn in the coming weeks. They also will go door to door along Maroon Drive collecting petition signatures.

"Everyone thinks education is about getting a good job, getting a good car," Verastegui said. "But it's really about improving your community. . . . We want people when they drive by Maroon Drive, we want them to think they can make a difference because he [Chavez] did." ❖

✳ **What is your reaction to Gloria Verastegui's campaign to name the street in front of her school Cesar Chavez Drive? What did reading this article make you think about?**

_____

_____

_____

_____

_____

✳ **Write a letter to your mayor or another town leader explaining an action you would like to take to help someone in your community or in the larger world. In the letter, describe the issue about which you are concerned. Discuss a possible action you and others can take to either solve the issue or make others aware of the problem.**

Date:

Dear   :

Yours truly,

Connect to what you are reading by using the information to help you and others take action on an issue or problem.

Examining Multiple Perspectives

You know from your own life experiences that there are many sides to every story. Did one friend ever tell you a one version of an event, only to have another friend report a different version? Different versions depend on the perspective of the person describing the event. This does not mean that one version of the story is more correct than another. A reader can learn more about a subject by **examining multiple viewpoints**.

In this unit, you will read several different perspectives about the atomic bomb that dropped on Hiroshima, Japan, in 1945. You will examine multiple viewpoints and consider how each portrays the bombing in a different light. You can compile these multiple points of view to develop your understanding of what happened on that day and its significance to humanity.

16 CHOOSING A PERSPECTIVE

A journalist is a writer who is constantly looking at different **perspectives** on a topic. Journalists have a variety of roles: they can report the news, research various issues and people, write opinion pieces, and create documentaries about important events. How a journalist chooses to tell a story gives us some clues about what he or she hopes readers will learn. Sometimes they try to stay completely objective and report factually. Other times, they have a "slant" on a story because they have opinions about what has taken place. They want to share those ideas with their readers.

John Hersey was a war correspondent during World War II. As you read an excerpt from Hersey's book on the bombing of Hiroshima, record reactions and questions in your **Response Notes.**

from **Hiroshima** by John Hersey

At nearly midnight, the night before the bomb was dropped, an announcer on the city's radio station said that about two hundred B-29's were approaching southern Honshu and advised the population of Hiroshima to evacuate to their designated "safe areas." Mrs. Hatsuyo Nakamura, the tailor's widow, who lived in the section called Nobori-cho and who had long had a habit of doing as she was told, got her three children—a ten year-old boy, Toshio, an eight-year-old girl, Yaeko, and a five-year-old girl, Myeko—out of bed and dressed them and walked with them to the military area known as the East Parade Ground, on the northeast edge of the city. There she unrolled some mats and the children lay down on them. They slept until about two, when they were awakened by the roar of the planes going over Hiroshima.

As soon as the planes had passed, Mrs. Nakamura started back with her children. They reached home a little after two-thirty and she immediately turned on the radio, which, to her distress, was just then broadcasting a fresh warning. When she looked at the children and saw how tired they were, and when she thought of the number of trips they had made in past weeks, all to no purpose, to the East Parade Ground, she decided that in spite of the instructions on the radio, she simply could not face starting out all over again. She put the children in their bedrolls on the floor, lay down herself at three o'clock, and fell asleep at once, so soundly that when planes passed over later, she did not waken to their sound.

The siren jarred her awake at about seven. She arose, dressed quickly, and hurried to the house of Mr. Nakamoto, the head of her Neighborhood Association, and asked him what she should do. He said that she should

Response Notes

Did the people have any idea about what might happen?

remain at home unless an urgent warning—a series of intermittent blasts of the siren—was sounded. She returned home, lit the stove in the kitchen, set some rice to cook, and sat down to read that morning's Hiroshima *Chugoku.* To her relief, the all-clear sounded at eight o'clock. She heard the children stirring, so she went and gave each of them a handful of peanuts and told them to stay on their bedrolls, because they were tired from the night's walk. She had hoped that they would go back to sleep, but the man in the house directly to the south began to make a terrible hullabaloo of hammering, wedging, ripping, and splitting. The prefectural government, convinced, as everyone in Hiroshima was, that that the city would be attacked soon, had begun to press with threats and warnings for the completion of wide fire lanes, which, it was hoped, might act in conjunction with the rivers to localize any fires started by an incendiary raid; and the neighbor was reluctantly sacrificing his home to the city's safety. Just the day before, the prefecture had ordered all able-bodied girls from the secondary schools to spend a few days helping to clear these lanes, and they started work soon after the all-clear sounded. ❖

❋ In the excerpt above, Hersey describes the hours leading up to the bombing through the thoughts and actions of Mrs. Nakamura. Write a paragraph that describes what you learned from her perspective about the city of Hiroshima.

_____

_____

_____

_____

_____

_____

_____

_____

_____

_____

On page 56 is a factual account about Hiroshima at the time of the bombing. In your **Response Notes,** record questions and reactions.

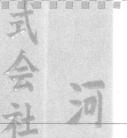
from **The Avalon Project** at Yale Law School

The center of the city contained a number of reinforced concrete buildings as well as lighter structures. Outside the center, the area was congested by a dense collection of small wooden workshops set among Japanese houses; a few larger industrial plants lay near the outskirts of the city. The houses were of wooden construction with tile roofs. Many of the industrial buildings also were of wood frame construction. The city as a whole was highly susceptible to fire damage.

Some of the reinforced concrete buildings were of a far stronger construction than is required by normal standards in America, because of the earthquake danger in Japan. This exceptionally strong construction undoubtedly accounted for the fact that the framework of some of the buildings, which were fairly close to the center of damage in the city, did not collapse.

The population of Hiroshima had reached a peak of over 380,000 earlier in the war but prior to the atomic bombing the population had steadily decreased because of a systematic evacuation ordered by the Japanese government. At the time of the attack the population was approximately 255,000. This figure is based on the registered population, used by the Japanese in computing ration quantities, and the estimates of additional workers and troops who were brought into the city may not be highly accurate. Hiroshima thus had approximately the same number of people as the city of Providence, R.I., or Dallas, Texas. ❖

✳ Discuss with a partner what you learned in this account.

✳ Describe the major differences in what you learned from each account.

_____

_____

_____

_____

_____

_____

_____

Consider why authors choose a particular perspective to write about a subject and what that might reveal about their purpose or "slant."

A moment in time is experienced differently by each person. Imagine that you were alive in 1945, right before the bombing of Hiroshima. If you were Mrs. Nakamura, you were at home with your children and thinking about their safety. If you were on your way to work, you might have heard loud engines and looked up at the sky to see a plane. If you were one hundred miles from Hiroshima, you might have seen the mushroom cloud before anything else. Each of these stories would have different **details** because each person's perspective on the subject is different.

In the section below, Hersey retells Mrs. Nakamura's experience as the bomb's impact is felt. In your **Response Notes,** record your reactions.

from **Hiroshima** by John Hersey

As Mrs. Nakamura stood watching her neighbor, everything flashed whiter than any white she had ever seen. She did not notice what happened to the man next door; the reflex of a mother set her in motion toward her children. She had taken a single step (the house was 1,350 yards, or three-quarters of a mile, from the center of the explosion) when something picked her up and she seemed to fly into the next room over the raised sleeping platform, pursued by parts of her house.

Timbers fell around her as she landed, and a shower of tiles pummeled her; everything became dark, for she was buried. The debris did not cover her deeply. She rose up and freed herself. She heard a child cry, "Mother, help me!," and saw her youngest—Myeko, the five-year-old—buried up to her breast and unable to move. As Mrs. Nakamura started frantically to claw her way toward the baby, she could see or hear nothing of her other children.

Response Notes

✳ Reread the excerpt and circle the three details that are most meaningful to you.

Response Notes

Continue reading Hersey's report from the perspective of another person. Use your **Response Notes** to record reactions and questions.

Miss Toshiko Sasaki, the East Asia Tin Works clerk, got up at three o'clock in the morning on the day the bomb fell. There was extra housework to do. Her eleven-month-old brother, Akio, had come down the day before with a serious stomach upset; her mother had taken him to the Tamura Pediatric Hospital and was staying there with him. Miss Sasaki, who was about twenty, had to cook breakfast for her father, a brother, a sister, and herself, and—since the hospital, because of the war, was unable to provide food—to prepare a whole day's meals for her mother and the baby, in time for her father, who worked in a factory making rubber earplugs for artillery crews, to take the food by on his way to the plant. When she had finished and had cleaned and put away the cooking things, it was nearly seven. The family lived in Koi, and she had a forty-five-minute trip to the tin works, in the section of town called Kannonmachi. She was in charge of the personnel records in the factory. She left Koi at seven, and as soon as she reached the plant, she went with some of the other girls from the personnel department to the factory auditorium. A prominent local Navy man, a former employee, had committed suicide the day before by throwing himself under a train—a death considered honorable enough to warrant a memorial service, which was to be held at the tin works at ten o'clock that morning. In the large hall, Miss Sasaki and the others made suitable preparations for the meeting. This work took about twenty minutes.

Miss Sasaki went back to her office and sat down at her desk. She was quite far from the windows, which were off to her left, and behind her were a couple of tall bookcases containing all the books of the factory library, which the personnel department had organized. She settled herself at her desk, put some things in a drawer, and shifted papers. She thought that before she began to make entries in her lists of new employee discharges, and departures for the Army, she would chat for a moment with the girl at her right. Just as she turned her head away from the windows, the room was filled with a blinding light. She was paralyzed by fear, fixed still in her chair for a long moment (the plant was 1,600 yards from the center).

Everything fell, and Miss Sasaki lost consciousness. The ceiling dropped suddenly and the wooden floor above collapsed in splinters and the people up there came down and the roof above them gave way; but principally and first of all, the bookcases right behind her swooped forward and the contents threw her down, with her left leg horribly twisted and breaking underneath her. There, in the tin factory, in the first moment of the atomic age, a human being was crushed by books. ❖

✳ Fill in the chart below to help you understand how Hersey uses details to reveal particular perspectives on the bombing.

Details of the incident	What the incident reveals
Mrs. Nakamura's Account ✳ *Rushes toward her children* ✳ ✳ ✳ ✳	✳ *Her children are always on her mind.* ✳ ✳ ✳ ✳
Miss Sasaki's Account ✳ *Father makes rubber earplugs* ✳ ✳ ✳ ✳	✳ *Many jobs were related to the war.* ✳ ✳ ✳ ✳

✳ Explain why you think Hersey chose to tell the story focused on the perspectives of those who experienced the bombing rather than writing a strictly factual account.

_____

_____

_____

_____

✳ Based on the excerpts, write what you think Hersey wants you to understand about the bombing of Hiroshima. List the details in his writing that lead you to this understanding.

_____

_____

_____

_____

Examine the details used to describe events and people in order to better understand the opinions and the perspective of a narrator or writer.

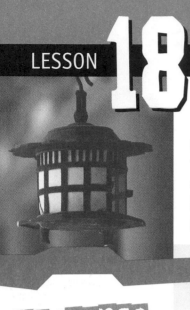

Sometimes the best way to find out information about an event is to talk to someone who was actually there. **Eyewitnesses** often give dramatic and detailed accounts. They rely on their memory to record the events. In the excerpt below, you will read how a survivor of the Hiroshima bombing felt and what he saw at the moment the bomb exploded. Circle words that reveal Hara's attitude toward the bombing.

Response Notes

from "**Summer Flower**" by Tamiki Hara in *The Crazy Iris and Other Stories of the Atomic Aftermath* edited by Kenzaburo Oe

My life was saved because I was in the bathroom. On the morning of August 6th, I had gotten up around eight o'clock. The air-raid alarm had sounded twice the night before and nothing had happened, so that before dawn I had taken off my clothes and slept in my night robe, which I had not put on for a long time. Such being the case, I had on only my shorts when I got up. My younger sister, when she saw me, complained of my rising late, but I went into the bathroom without replying.

I do not remember how many seconds passed after that. All of a sudden, a powerful blow struck me and darkness fell before my eyes. Involuntarily I shouted and held my hands over my head. Aside from the sound of something like the crashing of a storm, I could not tell what it was in the complete darkness. I groped for the door, opened it, and found the veranda. Until then, I had been hearing my own voice exclaiming, "Wah!" amid the rushing sounds, agonized at not being able to see. But after I came out to the veranda, the scene of destruction gradually loomed in the dusk before my eyes and I became clearly conscious.

It looked like an episode from a (loathsome dream.) At first, when the blow struck my head, and I lost my sight, I knew that I had not been killed. Then I became angry, thinking that things had become very troublesome. And my own shouts sounded almost like the voice of somebody else. But when I could see, vaguely as it was, the things around me, I felt as if I were standing stage center in a tragic play. Certainly I had beheld such a scene in a movie. Beyond the clouds of dust, patches of blue sky began to come into view. Light came in through holes in the walls and from other unexpected directions. As I walked gingerly on the boards where the tatami flooring had been blown off, my sister came rushing toward me. "You weren't hurt? You weren't hurt? Are you all right? Your eyes are bleeding. Go wash right away." She told me that there was still water running in the kitchen scullery.

Loathsome is a powerful word of hatred.

✳ Based on what this eyewitness has said so far, what is different about this perspective and the Hersey accounts?

_____

_____

_____

Continue reading Tamiki Hara's account. Keep track of your reactions in your **Response Notes.**

My brother had been seated at a table in his office when a flash of light raced through the garden. The next instant, he was blown some distance from his seat and for a while found himself squirming around under the wreckage of the house. At last he discovered an opening and succeeded in crawling out. From the direction of the factory he could hear the student workers screaming for help, and he went off to do what he could to rescue them.

My sister had seen the flash of light from the entrance hall and had rushed as fast as she could to hide under the stairs. As a result, she had suffered little injury.

Everyone had at first thought that just his own house had been hit by a bomb. But when they went outside and saw that it was the same everywhere, they were dumfounded. They were also greatly puzzled by the fact that, although the houses and other buildings had all been damaged or destroyed, there didn't seem to be any holes where the bombs had fallen. The air raid warning had been lifted, and shortly after that there had been a big flash of light and a soft hissing sound like magnesium burning. The next they knew everything was turned upside down. It was all like some kind of magical trick, my sister said, trembling with terror. ❖

✳ On the arms of the web, write information that you learned from Tamiki Hara's eyewitness account.

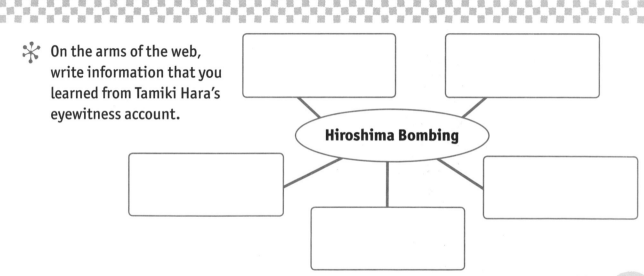

Hiroshima Bombing

※ Imagine that you are a reporter for your school newspaper. You want to give your classmates information about the lessons to be learned from the Hiroshima bombing. There is one person in your community, Tamika Hara, who was an eyewitness to the events. He introduces you to Mrs. Nakamura and Miss Sasaki, who are also survivors. You interview the three of them. Write a short article in which you describe the events. Incorporate quotations and details from the survivors.

WINFORD SCHOOL NEWS

VOL X   OCTOBER 11, 2006

HIROSHIMA REMEMBERED

Determine how eyewitness accounts contribute important perspectives that add to your understanding of an event.

Readers sometimes examine different points of view to gather as many perspectives as they can. As a reader, this might seem like completing a puzzle, since the versions of a story may come from several different sources.

The excerpt below is from the book *Shockwave* by Stephen Walker. The author uses interviews with various participants and survivors of the events to recreate the Hiroshima bombing inside the airplane that carried the atomic bomb. In this particular passage, you will add the pilots' perspective to your other viewpoints. Tom Ferebee and Paul Tibbets were the pilots on the *Enola Gay*, named for Tibbets's mother. As you read from the perspective of those inside the plane, keep track of your questions and reactions.

from **Shockwave** by Stephen Walker

Response Notes

Now Tibbets took control of the *Enola Gay*, switching off the C-1 autopilot for the last time until the bomb run. Behind him Van Kirk logged the height: they were level at 31,000 feet, their final bombing altitude. Outside the bomber's pressurized hull the temperature was minus twenty-four degrees centigrade, as cold as an Arctic winter, only far more inhospitable. Without oxygen a man would last less than two minutes out there. The sun glared through the windows. They were so high that the skies above them were a deep, burning indigo-blue. Far below, between the gaps in the clouds, the enemy coast slipped by: the flat, unwrinkled ocean suddenly giving way to a strip of land, a muddy carpet of parched browns and greens and hills and the occasional town sparkling in a shaft of sunlight. It looked almost peaceful down there.

Inside *Enola Gay's* waist section, Jake Beser concentrated over his electronic monitoring equipment, intensively searching every enemy frequency for possible interference with the bomb's radars: the result could be catastrophic. So far there was nothing. The air, he said, was "as clean as a hound's tooth." But Beser could also hear a whine through his headphones, and he knew what that meant. The Japanese early warning radar had locked onto the strike force. They were tracking the American bombers across Shikoku.

On the other side of the thirty-foot pressurized tunnel, Deak Parsons stared at the bomb console. All the green lights were still steady. If the enemy attacked now, he would have to act very quickly. Typically, he had already worked out exactly what needed to be done. He called it "responding to possible abnormal events." "Possible abnormal events" included such things as being shot down, in which case Parsons would somehow have to climb back into the freezing, unpressurized hell of the bomb bay, dismantle the breech plug with his domestic wrench (another sixteen turns) while the aircraft was screaming or shaking or hurtling to the ground, and disarm the bomb. If he failed, the bomb would almost certainly explode. If they were forced to ditch, it would also very likely explode, since tests in Los Alamos had already demonstrated that seawater leaking into *Little Boy's* casing had an unfortunate tendency to initiate a chain reaction. Parsons had designed as many fail-safes into the bomb as was possible—it could even be dropped if only the pilot and he survived an attack—but in truth there were an infinite number of possible abnormal events, and it was impossible to provide against all of them. In his pocket was a list of coded messages he would shortly use to transmit the result of the drop back to Tinian. There were twenty-eight alternatives on the list. The twenty-fifth was *Returning with unit to indicated place due to damage to aircraft.* If only it were that simple.

Alone in *Enola Gay's* tail, isolated in his capsule from the rest of the crew, Bob Caron stared out at the sky. Despite his sunglasses the glare burned into his eyes. Beneath his windscreen the two .50-caliber machine guns projected into the slipstream. As they approached the enemy coast he had attempted to struggle into his flak suit, but the turret was too cramped. His one protection against anti-aircraft fire lay in a heap on the floor. Now he began scanning every inch of the sky for enemy fighters, mentally tearing it into strips and rigorously examining each strip, up and down, left to right, strip by strip, searching for the dot that could suddenly turn into a fighter and kill you. But there were no dots. The only aircraft out there were American: *The Great Artiste* and *Dimples 91*, hanging off the tail a few hundred feet behind. Otherwise the sky was empty.

Up front, Tibbets also scanned the empty sky. Back in Europe they used to say the antiaircraft fire was so thick you could get out and walk on it. But Shikoku's coastal batteries were silent. No bursts of shrapnel-filled flak greeted them as they crossed the island. The landscape unrolled harmlessly below. Tibbets was convinced that his policy of sending individual or small formations of his bombers to the Empire was paying off. The enemy were simply ignoring them. The three bombers rode the skies undisturbed, the southerly wind pushing them along at 328 mph—well over five miles a minute—toward their target. Van Kirk passed a new estimate to Tibbets. They would reach their initial point—the start of the bomb run—at exactly 0912. "I was trying to hit it exactly," he said. "By this time it was a game for me." Game or not, he suddenly glanced up, looking past

the two pilots and through the glass nose. Something glinted on the horizon, a good fifty miles away, beyond Shikoku and across the Inland Sea. He stared in fascination. It was unmistakably a city. ❖

✳ Write a paragraph that describes your reactions to reading the perspectives of people inside the plane. Use quotes from the passage that influence your reactions.

_____

_____

_____

_____

_____

_____

_____

_____

_____

✳ Imagine that some months after the bombing one of the *Enola Gay* pilots meets a Hiroshima survivor. What reactions might they have to each other when they meet? Write a possible dialogue between one of the pilots and one of the survivors.

_____

_____

_____

_____

_____

_____

_____

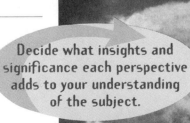

Decide what insights and significance each perspective adds to your understanding of the subject.

Historical fiction allows an author to use elements of history to create a believable version of real events. Laurence Yep uses the events of Hiroshima to tell the story of Sachi, a fictional combination of several school children. As you read, make comparisons between this account and the nonfiction passages in earlier lessons. In your **Response Notes,** record reactions and questions.

Response Notes

from **Hiroshima** by Laurence Yep

Sachi wakes a few minutes later when she hears someone screaming. At first, there is so much smoke and dust she feels as if she is staring at a black wall. Then the smoke and dust rise like a curtain. She is stunned when she sees all the damage. One moment there was a city here. Now all the buildings are destroyed. The streets are filled with rubble and ruins. She does not know what could cause such wide destruction.

Shocked, Sachi stumbles through the wasteland until she stops upon a lawn. From the wrecked buildings, people call for help. Before she can help anyone, the buildings go up in flames.

It is so hot around her that the grass catches fire. She crouches down and waits and hopes. The sheet of fire retreats. Flames shoot out of the nearby houses. People continue to scream. Everywhere, there is a sea of fire.

Sachi follows some people as they run into a cemetery. She jumps over tombstones. The pine trees around them catch fire with a great crackling noise.

Ahead she sees a river. People jump into it to get away from the fire. In the panic, some people are crushed. Others drown. Sachi cannot swim. She jumps in anyway. Then she sees a wooden bucket drifting by. She grabs it and holds it desperately.

Soon the water is full of bodies.

The hot ash from all the fires soars high, high into the sky. When the fiery ash mixes with the cold air, it causes rain. It is a horrible kind of rain.

The rain falls in drops as big as marbles. The drops are black and greasy with dust. The drops sting like falling pebbles.

The rain leaves black, oily spots wherever it falls.

The rain is radioactive. It will make people sick, too. They will also die.

After about an hour, the rain puts out the fires. Somebody finds Sachi and brings her to the hospital.

The people living just outside Hiroshima think they are safe. They search through the deadly wasteland for family and friends. They do not know about radiation. Some of these searchers will also fall ill. Many of them will die. ❖

✳ What new information did you learn from this fictional account?

_____

_____

_____

_____

✳ The excerpts in this unit offer you a variety of perspectives on
the bombing of Hiroshima. In the chart below, evaluate each.
Indicate the strengths and limitations of each point of view.
Focus on what you learned from each account.

Excerpt from	Strengths	Weaknesses
Mrs. Nakamura's account		
The Avalon Project's factual account		
Miss Sasaki's account		
Pilot's account		
Sachi's fictional account		

✳ Think of an eventful experience in your life that occurred on what seemed an otherwise normal day. Imagine that a newspaper reporter is trying to capture for a magazine story your perspective of that day and the event. Since a reporter is writing your story, this is not a first-person "I" version. It more closely resembles how Hersey treated Mrs. Nakamura's and Miss Sasaki's accounts. Be sure to include a description of your actions before, during, and after the event.

_____

_____

_____

_____

_____

_____

_____

_____

_____

_____

_____

_____

_____

_____

_____

_____

_____

_____

_____

Evaluate the strengths and limitations of each perspective to understand how it adds to your understanding of the subject.

Focusing on Language and Craft

Once you have command of the basic skills of reading and writing, you can attend to the **art of language: style and structure.** You know the differences style in clothes can make; style affects the way you act and how others respond to you. It is the same with language. An **author's style** makes us want to read or not read. Style makes what we read interesting, difficult, funny, or moving. However, style is not the entire issue; the other part is structure. To know how a particular outfit is going to look on you, you have to put it on. A style that looks good on one person may look silly on another.

In this unit, you will learn about some of the features of language that create style and structure. You'll see them in the texts you read, both in poems and in prose. You'll also try to create different structures as you experiment with new ways to develop your own writing style.

LESSON 21 USING OPPOSITES TO CREATE STRUCTURE

Our language is filled with opposites. Opposition finds its way into stories, television shows, music lyrics, and movies. Almost every story has a balance between opposite poles. Just for fun, see how many pairs of opposites you can come up with in two minutes. We've written a couple of obvious ones to help you get started. How many pairs can you think of? You will use your list later.

hot   cold   up   down

true   false

Eve Merriam uses opposition to create a series of similes that make a statement in her poem "Simile: Willow and Ginkgo." The use of figurative language like similes is one way writers define their styles. Read the poem, which uses two trees, the willow and the gingko, as the basis of comparison. Underline the similes.

Response Notes

Simile: Willow and Ginkgo by Eve Merriam

The willow is like an etching,
Fine-lined against the sky.
The ginkgo is like a crude sketch,
Hardly worthy to be signed.
The willow's music is like a soprano
Delicate and thin.
The ginkgo's tune is like a chorus
With everyone joining in.
The willow is sleek as a velvet-nosed calf;
The ginkgo is leathery as an old bull.
The willow's branches are like silken thread;
The ginkgo's like stubby rough wool.
The willow is like a nymph with streaming hair;
Wherever it grows, there is green and gold and fair.
The willow dips to the water,
Protected and precious, like the king's favorite daughter.

The ginkgo forces its way through gray concrete:
Like a city child, it grows up in the street.
Thrust against the metal sky,
Somehow it survives and even thrives.
My eyes feast upon the willow,
But my heart goes to the ginkgo.

Sketch the two trees using words and phrases from the poem to guide your drawing. Try including some of the words as part of your drawings. Choose one shape for the willow and another for the ginkgo.

Name of tree ____________	Name of tree ____________

Talk with your partner or group about the characteristics of the two trees. It is clear that the narrator of the poem prefers one to the other. Which one do you prefer? Why?

____

SIMILES

You have probably written and studied similes many times already, but this is an easy poem that makes the concept clear. A **simile** is a particular kind of **metaphor,** or comparison of two unlike things. The *simile* depends on the use of *like* or *as* for its comparison.

✳️ In the **Response Notes,** use arrows or lines to show what two things are being compared. For example, you might draw an arrow from *willow* to *etching.*

STRUCTURE OR FORM

✳️ Notice how this poem alternates between the two trees. Underline all lines referring to the willow. Then look at how Merriam shifts back and forth between the willow and the gingko. What lines tell you that the narrator of the poem felt drawn to the gingko?

_____

_____

_____

✳️ Look at your list of opposites. Using the list as a starting point, divide your list of pairs into those that refer to *things* and those that are *abstract,* like values. For example, *willow* and *gingko* refer to things, whereas *good* and *bad* refer to abstract qualities.

Pairs referring to things	Pairs referring to abstract ideas
Examples: *willow, gingko* *hill, valley*	*Examples:* *good, bad* *right, wrong*

✳ Which pairs of words in the poem refer to things? _____

✳ Which pairs refer to abstract ideas? _____

✳ What abstract ideas might the willow stand for? _____

✳ What abstract ideas might the gingko stand for? _____

✳ Choose one pair of *things* and write your own poem titled
"Simile: _____ and _____ ." Follow Merriam's poem
loosely by first describing one of your "things" and then the other.
Conclude your poem as Merriam did by stating which of the two your
"heart goes to."

       Simile: _____ and _____

Comparing opposites
is one way to structure
a poem.

ne poet whose **style** is easily recognized is e. e. cummings. One mark of his style is that he never capitalized his name and rarely capitalized words in his poems. Cummings loved to play with the idea of opposites. The opposition in this next poem is not as obvious as it is in Eve Merriam's poem "Simile: Willow and Gingko," but you will find it in almost every line. Note as you read or listen to this poem how cummings "plays" with language in his poetry.

✳ Use the **Response Notes** column to make observations about the poem.

- Comment on any ideas you have about the meaning as you read.

- Note the instances of opposites that occur in the poem.

- Make notes about what you observe regarding the form of the poem. When you read this poem, suspend your expectations about conventional punctuation, capitalization, and the way words are used. Look particularly at these elements:
  * **rhyme**
  * **capitalization** (Yes, there is one word capitalized twice. Why?)
  * **punctuation** (Did you notice the period? What point does it serve?)
  * **parts of speech** (Notice how words don't fit into their usual parts of speech. Make notes about words that are used in unusual ways. For example, "he sang his *didn't* he danced his *did*.")

anyone lived in a pretty how town by e.e. cummings

anyone lived in a pretty how town
(with up so floating many bells down)
spring summer autumn winter
he sang his didn't he danced his did

Women and men (both little and small)
cared for anyone not at all
they sowed their isn't they reaped their same
sun moon stars rain

children guessed (but only a few
and down they forgot as up they grew
autumn winter spring summer)
that noone loved him more by more

when by now and tree by leaf
she laughed his joy she cried his grief
bird by snow and stir by still
anyone's any was all to her

someones married their everyones
laughed their cryings and did their dance
(sleep wake hope and then) they
said their nevers they slept their dream

stars rain sun moon
(and only the snow can begin to explain
how children are apt to forget to remember
with up so floating many bells down)

one day anyone died i guess
(and noone stooped to kiss his face)
busy folk buried them side by side
little by little and was by was

all by all and deep by deep
and more by more they dream their sleep
noone and anyone earth by april
wish by spirit and if by yes.

Women and men (both dong and ding)
summer autumn winter spring
reaped their sowing and went their came
sun moon stars rain ❖

TOWN
SPEED
LIMIT
30

WRITING YOUR INTERPRETATION

✳ Many people have written long explanations about this poem. Some people think that *anyone* and *noone* represent a man and a woman and that the seasons, stars, and weather represent the passages of their lives.

Write what this poem means to you. As you write, use words, phrases, or whole lines from the poem to support what you say. Remember that there is no right answer to the question, but it is important to have good reasons for what you say. When you finish, share your writing with one or more classmates. How many interpretations are there?

_____

_____

_____

_____

_____

_____

_____

_____

_____

_____

_____

_____

_____

_____

_____

_____

By suspending your expectations regarding the use of language, you become open to many possible interpretations.

S tyle is as much about **sound** as it is about imagery. Listen to the rhythm of the sledgehammer in the poem. Turpin combined the worlds of being a construction worker by day and a poet by night. He writes that he likes the attention to detail, to rhythm, both on the construction site and in his poems.

Read the poem. Use the **Response Notes** to write the questions you have about what some words or lines mean. Do any lines catch your interest?

Sledgehammer Song by Mark Turpin

The way you hold the haft,
The way it climbs a curve,
A manswung curve,
The way it undoes what was done.
The way a stake sinks,
Cement splits or a stud
Spins off its nails.

The way shoulders shrug.
The way the breezes waft
And wake and tease a cheek,
The way it undoes what was done.
The way a cabinet cracks
And rakes and bares
The nail-scarred wall beneath.

The way a stance is spread,
The way the steel head pings
And thrums and thuds,
The way it undoes what was done.
The way a bathtub breaks:
Pieces barrowed, porcelain
Left in a bin.

The way sight is stark.
The way the weight wills the arms,
The back and heart,
The way it undoes what was done.
The way the weight is weighed,
Stalling the swing,
The sorrow mid-arc. ❖

Response Notes

INTERPRETATION

✳ The last four lines seem to go beyond the act of swinging the sledgehammer to something more internal. We have no way of really knowing what the poet means by those lines, but perhaps you can make a good guess. What could he mean by "the sorrow mid-arc"? Try to explain what those lines might mean.

_____

_____

_____

WRITING A POEM USING SOUNDS

Think about the sounds in your life, repetitive sounds. What things do you hear over and over? Does the music you listen to have a repetitive beat? Do you like to hear the sounds of a particular sport? (Think of tennis, for instance. If you watch it on television without the sound, it is hard to follow the ball.) Try to isolate some of the sounds that fill your daily life and write a short poem using those sounds. You might use Turpin's way of beginning each line with "The way . . ."

_____

_____

_____

_____

_____

_____

_____

_____

_____

_____

_____

_____

_____

_____

Style can be composed of sounds as well as images.

Style is all about choice: what words and sentences to use; whether to use dialogue; how to use description, figurative language, and tone. The **structure** of a piece of writing is the way it is put together. Structure is the arrangement of words into sentences and sentences into paragraphs. In the next two lessons, you will analyze the style and structure of short excerpts by John Steinbeck and Judith Ortiz Cofer.

When you are asked to analyze an author's *style,* you might start by thinking about the author's word choices. Use the **Response Notes** column to comment on these questions:

1 Is the author's language formal or informal?

2 Is the author's vocabulary simple or complex or somewhere in between?

3 Does the author use sensory language—that is, words that can help you see, hear, touch, smell, or taste the thing described?

Read the following selection by John Steinbeck. In this excerpt from *The Pearl,* you will read about a tense moment.

from **The Pearl** by John Steinbeck

Response Notes

The sun was warming the brush house, breaking through its crevices in long streaks. And one of the streaks fell on the hanging box where Coyotito lay, and on the ropes that held it.

It was a tiny movement that drew their eyes to the hanging box. Kino and Juana froze in their positions. Down the rope that hung the baby's box from the roof support a scorpion moved slowly. His stinging tail was straight out behind him, but he could whip it up in a flash of time.

Kino's breath whistled in his nostrils and he opened his mouth to stop it. And then the startled look was gone from him and the rigidity from his body. In his mind a new song had come, the Song of Evil, the music of the enemy, of any foe of the family, a savage, secret, dangerous melody, and underneath, the Song of the Family cried plaintively.

The scorpion moved delicately down the rope toward the box. Under her breath Juana repeated an ancient magic to guard against such evil, and on top of that she muttered a Hail Mary between clenched teeth. But Kino was in motion. His body glided quietly across the room, noiselessly and smoothly. His hands were in front of him, palms down, and his eyes were on the scorpion. Beneath it in the hanging box Coyotito laughed and reached up his hand toward it. It sensed danger when Kino was almost within reach of it. It stopped, and its tail rose up over its back in little jerks and the curved thorn on the tail's end glistened.

Kino stood perfectly still. He could hear Juana whispering the old magic again, and he could hear the evil music of the enemy. He could not move until the scorpion moved, and it felt for the source of the death that was coming to it. Kino's hand went forward very slowly, very smoothly. The thorned tail jerked upright. And at that moment the laughing Coyotito shook the rope and the scorpion fell.

Kino's hand leaped to catch it, but it fell past his fingers, fell on the baby's shoulder, landed and struck. Then, snarling, Kino had it, had it in his fingers, rubbing it to a paste in his hands. He threw it down and beat it into the earth floor with his fist, and Coyotito screamed with pain in his box. But Kino beat and stamped the enemy until it was only a fragment and a moist place in the dirt. His teeth were bared and fury flared in his eyes and the Song of the Enemy roared in his ears. ❖

✳ Write a sentence that describes the atmosphere you think Steinbeck creates in this small section from *The Pearl*.

_____

_____

_____

Read the excerpt from an essay by Judith Ortiz Cofer. In the **Response Notes** column, respond to the questions about word choice listed on page 79.

from "The Story of My Body" by Judith Ortiz Cofer

I was born a white girl in Puerto Rico but became a brown girl when I came to live in the United States. My Puerto Rican relatives called me tall; at the American school, some of my rougher classmates called me Skinny Bones, and the Shrimp because I was the smallest member of my classes all through grammar school until high school, when the midget Gladys was given the honorary post of front row center for class pictures and scorekeeper, bench warmer, in P. E. I reached my full stature of five feet in sixth grade.

I started out life as a pretty baby and learned to be a pretty girl from a pretty mother. Then at ten years of age I suffered one of the worst cases of chicken pox I have ever heard of. My entire body, including the inside of my ears and in between my toes, was covered with pustules which in a fit of panic at my appearance I scratched off my face, leaving permanent scars. A cruel school nurse told me I would always have them—tiny cuts that looked as if a mad cat had plunged its claws deep into my skin. I grew my hair long and hid behind it for the first years of my adolescence. This was when I learned to be invisible. ❖

✳ Explain how you think Cofer became "invisible" in this excerpt from "The Story of My Body."

_____

_____

_____

✳ Use the Venn diagram below to compare Steinbeck's and Cofer's word choices. On the lines marked *e.g.* (*e.g.* means "for example"), give examples from the writing to support your decisions.

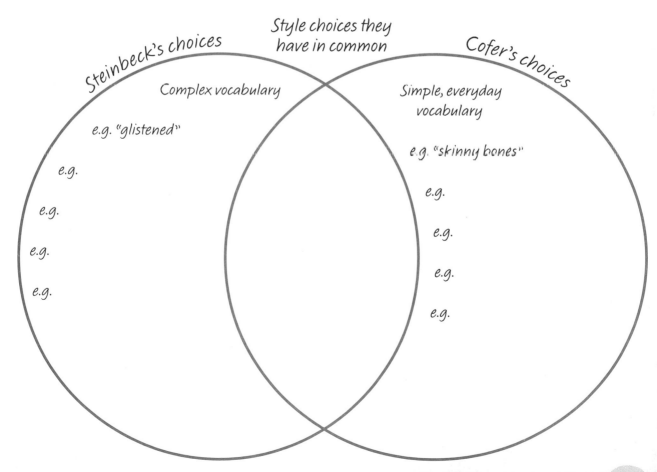

Steinbeck's choices

Style choices they have in common

Cofer's choices

Complex vocabulary

e.g. "glistened"

e.g.

e.g.

e.g.

e.g.

Simple, everyday vocabulary

e.g. "skinny bones"

e.g.

e.g.

e.g.

e.g.

✳ Write a comparison of the kinds of word choices Steinbeck and Cofer make. Tell why you think each author chose these kinds of words.

_____

_____

_____

_____

_____

_____

_____

_____

_____

Word choice is one of the most important aspects of an author's style. Developing your vocabulary will give you more options in creating your own style.

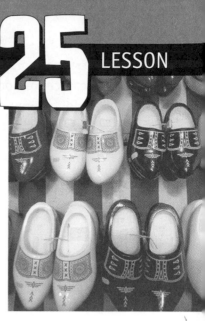

There are many elements, in addition to word choice, that play an important role in an author's style. **Style** involves the way an author uses

- sentence length;
- description;
- figurative language (similes and metaphors, for example);
- tone.

✳ Fill in the Venn diagram with notes about the elements of style listed above.

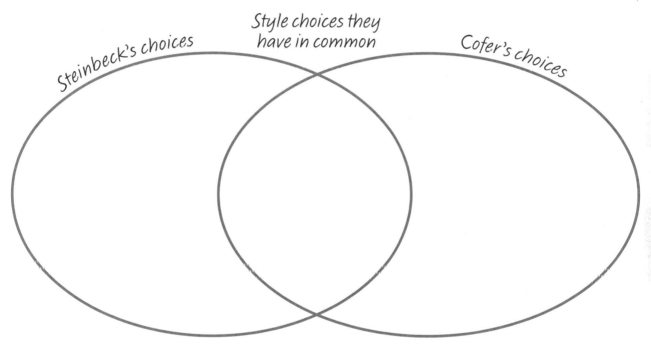

Steinbeck's choices   Style choices they have in common   Cofer's choices

Think about style as evidence of personality; not just the personality of the author, but the personality of the narrator or even the personality of a place. That may sound strange, but if you reread the Steinbeck excerpt, you will see that he has created an atmosphere of the place, which you might think of as its personality. Cofer has created the sense of a young girl whose self-image changes.

Review the lessons in this unit as you think about choices writers make in style and structure. Think about your own writing, the choices you make when you look at your first drafts and want to improve them.

Write a short piece of your own, either a poem or a descriptive piece of prose. You can choose one of the literature pieces you have read in this unit to use as a model for your own poem or prose paragraph. When you finish, exchange your *Daybook* with another student and read each other's writing with an eye for style and structure.

_____

_____

_____

_____

_____

_____

_____

_____

_____

_____

_____

_____

_____

_____

_____

_____

_____

_____

_____

_____

_____

_____

_____

_____

Understanding the style and structure of a poem or prose piece gives you more options in your own writing.

Studying an Author

If I read a book and it makes my whole body so cold no fire can ever warm me, I know *that* is poetry. If I feel physically as if the top of my head were taken off, I know *that* is poetry. These are the only ways I know it. Is there any other way?

Emily Dickinson

In this author study, you will experience some of Emily Dickinson's best-loved poems. Almost unknown as a poet in her lifetime, **Emily Dickinson** is now recognized as one of America's greatest poets and, in the view of some, one of the greatest lyric poets of all time. Emily Dickinson was a passionate poet. She chose to live a secluded life, living within the confines of the family home, the garden, and a small circle of family and friends. Within that seclusion, she felt deeply, wrote with sensitivity, and imagined with intensity. These are the qualities Emily Dickinson shared in her poetry and in her letters.

26 MAKING ABSTRACT IDEAS CONCRETE

Poets choose their words carefully to convey their ideas effectively and economically. Notice how Emily Dickinson uses **concrete images** to express her thoughts about certain **abstract ideas.** Listen to someone read the poem aloud or read it yourself. In the **Response Notes,** capture your initial response by writing or drawing.

Response Notes

Poem #288 by Emily Dickinson

I'm Nobody! Who are you?
Are you—Nobody—Too?
Then there's a pair of us!
Don't tell! they'd advertise—you know!

How dreary—to be—Somebody!
How public—like a Frog—
To tell one's name—the livelong June—
To an admiring Bog! ❖

✳ Write what the poem seems to be about.

_____

_____

✳ Read the poem again. Make some notes about the following elements of the poem. Discuss your ideas with a partner.

■ Dickinson's use of punctuation and capitalization

_____

■ words that are unfamiliar to you

_____

■ words you know but are used in unfamiliar ways

_____

■ connections you made with the meaning of the poem

_____

■ other elements you noticed about the poem

_____

MAKING AN ABSTRACTION CONCRETE

Poetry uses the poetic device of **metaphor** to make abstract concepts—like *friendship, love, fear,* or *hope*—concrete by relating them to things that we can touch, see, taste, feel, and hear. In this next poem, Dickinson takes a common abstraction—*hope*—and makes it concrete. You may have read the first line of the next poem as it often appears on greeting cards.

Poem #254 by Emily Dickinson

"Hope" is the thing with feathers—
That perches in the soul—
And sings the tune without the words—
And never stops—at all—

And sweetest—in the Gale—is heard—
And sore must be the storm—
That could abash the little Bird
That kept so many warm—

I've heard it in the chillest land—
And on the strangest Sea—
Yet, never, in Extremity,
It asked a crumb—of Me. ❖

Response Notes

✳ Write what you think the poem is about.

_____

_____

✳ As you did before, make some notes about the poem to share with a partner.

■ Does this poem "speak" to you? If so, talk about what it "says."

_____

■ What do you think about Dickinson's metaphor "hope is a thing with feathers"?

_____

- Are you getting comfortable with Dickinson's use of the dash instead of other punctuation? How does it affect the way you read the poem?

_____

_____

- What about capitalization? Why do you think she capitalized words such as *Gale, Bird, Sea, Extremity,* and *Me*?

_____

_____

- Why do you think the poet does not title her poems, but numbers them instead?

_____

_____

MAKING ANOTHER ABSTRACTION CONCRETE

✳ With a partner or your group, make a list of abstractions that are important to you. Then follow these steps to write a poem.

- Choose an abstract idea.
- Make it concrete by drawing or sketching something that you think stands for this abstraction. If you were writing the "hope" poem, you could draw a bird of some kind, perhaps an angelic bird, since it "perches in the soul."
- Using concrete terms, write at least a four-line stanza about your abstraction. If you have a good idea in progress, write more.
- Share your poem with a partner.

_____

_____

_____

_____

_____

Concrete images help us understand abstract ideas.

Good readers always **make connections** when they read. As you read the next two poems, think about your own responses as well as the connections that exist between what you are reading, what you have experienced, and other works you have read. Use the **Response Notes** column to record any connections you make as you read these poems.

Poem #919 by Emily Dickinson

If I can stop one Heart from breaking
I shall not live in vain
If I can ease one Life the Aching
Or cool one Pain

Or help one fainting Robin
Unto his Nest again
I shall not live in Vain. ❖

Poem #435 by Emily Dickinson

Much Madness is divinest Sense—
To a discerning Eye—
Much Sense—the starkest Madness—
'Tis the Majority
In this, as All, prevail—
Assent—and you are sane—
Demur—you're straightway dangerous—
And handled with a Chain— ❖

Response Notes

❋ Discuss these poems with a partner or in a small group. Talk about any difficulties you have in understanding them. Then talk about the connections you made to these two poems.

IMPRESSIONS OF DICKINSON'S POETRY SO FAR

❋ Using your own responses as well as what you learned from your discussions, complete the ten sentences on page 90 with what you know about Dickinson's poetry.

1   Emily Dickinson writes about _____

      _____

2   Dickinson's poems make me feel _____

      _____

3   I had the strongest reaction to _____

      _____

4   Much of Dickinson's imagery is taken from _____

      _____

5   The strongest image for me is _____

      _____

6   I didn't understand _____

      _____

7   What I wonder about is _____

      _____

8   The poet used some words I didn't know. I wonder what

      _____ means.

9   Dickinson's use of rhyme is _____

      _____

10   Of these four poems, the poem I like best is _____
      because _____

✳ In your group, compare your responses to the statements. List
   any questions you have about Dickinson's poems.

_____

_____

_____

_____

> Making and sharing
> personal connections to the
> words and ideas of poems helps
> us understand the meaning.

28 LESSON

Read or listen to poem #585, "I Like to See It Lap the Miles." Do a quick-write or a quick-draw in the **Response Notes** column to solidify your first impression of this poem.

Poem #585 by Emily Dickinson

I like to see it lap the Miles—
And lick the Valleys up—
And stop to feed itself at Tanks—
And then—prodigious step

Around a Pile of Mountains—
And supercilious peer
In Shanties—by the sides of Roads—
And then a Quarry pare

To fit its Ribs
And crawl between
Complaining all the while
In horrid—hooting stanza—
The chase itself down Hill—

And neigh like Boanerges—
Then—punctual as a Star
Stop—docile and omnipotent
At its own stable door— ❖

Response Notes

In "Hope Is the Thing with Feathers" (Poem #254), you dealt with one of Dickinson's metaphors. Sometimes a metaphor deals with two concrete things rather than an abstraction like *hope*. Poem #585 makes use of an extended metaphor, a comparison between *it* in line one, which seems like a horse, and a train.

Chad Walsh, a man who has written extensively about poetry, suggests the exercise on page 92, which will help you explore the metaphor in Poem #585. Rewrite the poem with an *elephant* as the implied comparison, instead of a *horse*.

❋ In the left column of the chart below write a list of all the words you would have to replace if you were to change the subject.

❋ In the middle column, list the words you would use if the horse were to become an elephant.

❋ In the right column, do the same thing as if the comparison were with a tiger.

Words in the original poem you would have to replace if you changed the subject	Elephant: words that you would substitute for the original "horse" words	Tiger: words that you would substitute for the original "horse" words

❋ On a separate sheet of paper, write the poem twice with your changes: first make the horse an elephant, then a tiger.

❋ Read your versions aloud to a partner, then listen to your partner's versions. Talk about how each of the different animal comparisons changed the poem.

■ Did any of the words you removed have a particular sound that made the train image work?

■ Has the tone changed?

■ Has the feeling changed?

■ Does it sound better, worse, or just different?

❋ Go back to the original horse image and note the qualities of the horse that Dickinson chose. (See the left column in the chart.) How does the horse image fit the train image that Dickinson develops in the poem?

CONVENTIONS IN EMILY DICKINSON'S POEMS

As you have probably noticed, Dickinson created her own rules of punctuation and capitalization. She used dashes almost as breathless pauses and capital letters to begin words that she thought were important, regardless of where they fell in a sentence.

While some of Dickinson's poems use true rhyme, most do not. Rather, Dickinson generally used what is now called *slant rhyme*, which is slightly "off" the complete or true rhyming sound. The critics of her time didn't know what to make of this eccentric woman who violated the traditional rules of poetry. In fact, when her family and a friend first published her poems after her death, they were "corrected" so that the poems had true rhymes and traditional punctuation and capitalization.

The rewritten poems appeared in print for many years after her death. It wasn't until 1955 that they were published the way she wrote them.

❋ Reread Poem #585, "I Like to See It Lap the Miles," then rewrite it with conventional punctuation and capitalization. If you can turn the *slant rhymes* into true rhymes, do that, too, but that is much harder to do. Write your "conventionally correct" version below. The first stanza has been done for you.

I like to see it lap the miles

and lick the valleys up

and stop to feed itself at tanks,

and then, prodigious, step

✳ Compare your version with that of a partner or those of others in your group.

✳ Write a short paragraph in which you discuss the different effects of the poem as Dickinson wrote it and as you have written it with traditional conventions. Comment on which version you like better and why.

_____

_____

_____

_____

_____

_____

_____

_____

_____

_____

_____

Understanding metaphor is basic to understanding meaning in poetry.

OUTWARD ASPECTS OF HER LIFE

The outward facts of Emily Dickinson's life are well known. She was born in 1830 in Amherst, Massachusetts, to a highly respected, prominent family. She was a middle child, devoted to her older brother Austin and her younger sister Lavinia. She was witty, had friends, and went to parties. She went away to college (now Mount Holyoke College), where she was successful but stayed only a year.

INWARD ASPECTS OF HER LIFE

When she returned to her family home in Amherst, she entered into an inward life that deepened into a strong reclusiveness. She loved people, but when they came to visit, she would frequently speak with them from behind a door that was slightly ajar. She also chose to wear only white, and neighborhood children would observe her when she would lower cookies to them on a rope from an upstairs window.

Emily Dickinson was a frequent letter writer. Letters were to Emily Dickinson what email is to people today. She began corresponding with family and friends when she was very young and continued until her death. When she became a recluse, rarely leaving her father's house, she kept up a heavy volume of letters. In her correspondence, she lived a rich life, not unlike the lives of many housebound people today who establish rich and rewarding relationships through the Internet. Her letters were filled with snippets of poetry, but, because her poetry was so strange for its day, readers didn't realize what a treasure it was.

One of the curiosities of Emily's life is that she published only seven of nearly 2,000 poems during her lifetime. The rest she tied in bundles and wrapped in blue ribbon with instructions to burn them after her death. Fortunately, her sister disobeyed her wishes and the poems were saved. Today she is acknowledged as one of the most gifted of all American poets.

✳ Work with a partner or in a small group to think of a list of questions you have about Emily Dickinson. You might wonder, for example, why she became a recluse or how she felt about her poetry.

_____

_____

_____

_____

A GRAPHIC VIEW OF EMILY DICKINSON

✳ Working individually, with a partner, or with your group, create a graphic to express your understanding of Emily Dickinson's life and the poems you have read. Use colored markers to construct your graphic on the next page.

- Choose a unifying symbol to stand for Emily Dickinson. Use this symbol as the organizing feature of your graphic.

- Use color, design, words, and additional symbols to organize your ideas about the poems and about her life.

- Your graphic should include all of the poems you have read, but you might want to feature one particular poem.

- Use some of Dickinson's own phrases or lines as part of the graphic.

- Use your own words, phrases, or sentences to enhance your graphic. You might use the sentences you wrote earlier in response to the poems or come up with new ideas.

- Give your graphic a title.

- Share your graphic with other members of the class and talk about your reasons for designing it the way that you did.

✳ Write a short analysis of your graphic. Explain how the symbols, colors, designs, and words work together to portray the meaning or effect of Dickinson's poems.

_____

_____

_____

_____

_____

_____

_____

Glimpses into an author's life can lead to a greater understanding of her or his work.

30

COMPARING AND CONTRASTING TWO POEMS

Sometimes reading two poems by different poets on a similar subject will add to your understanding of both poems. You can think about the subject from two perspectives. In this lesson, you are going to read two poems, the first by Emily Dickinson and the second by A. E. Housman. Use the **Response Notes** to comment on meaning and to capture your questions. Mark lines in the poems with which you make a connection.

Poem #67 by Emily Dickinson

Response Notes

Success is counted sweetest
By those who ne'er succeed.
To comprehend a nectar
Requires sorest need.

Not one of all the purple Host
Who took the Flag today
Can tell the definition
So clear of Victory

As he defeated—dying—
On whose forbidden ear
The distant strains of triumph
Burst agonized and clear! ✧

To an Athlete Dying Young by A.E. Housman

The time you won your town the race
We chaired you through the market-place;
Man and boy stood cheering by,
And home we brought you shoulder-high.

To-day, the road all runners come,
Shoulder-high we bring you home,
And set you at your threshold down,
Townsman of a stiller town.

Smart lad, to slip betimes away
From fields where glory does not stay
And early though the laurel grows
It withers quicker than the rose.

Eyes the shady night has shut
Cannot see the record cut,
And silence sounds no worse than cheers
After earth has stopped the ears:

Now you will not swell the rout
Of lads that wore their honours out,
Runners whom renown outran
And the name died before the man.

So set, before its echoes fade,
The fleet foot on the sill of shade,
And hold to the low lintel up
The still-defended challenge-cup.

And round that early-laurelled head
Will flock to gaze the strengthless dead,
And find unwithered on its curls
The garland briefer than a girl's. ❖

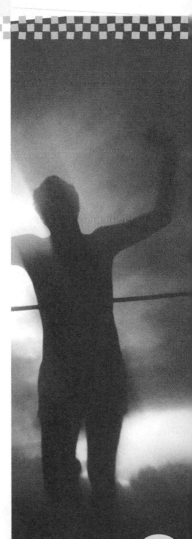

✳ Working with your partner or group, talk about both poems. Use questions 1-9 to start your discussion.

1 Who is the speaker of the poem? To whom is the poem addressed?

_____

_____

2 What is the setting? Is it real or abstract?

_____

_____

3 Is there action in the poem? What is it?

_____

_____

4 What is the form of the poem? Where does the poet depart from these patterns and forms? Why?

_____

5 What figures of speech does the poem contain—metaphor, simile, or personification?

_____

_____

6 What kinds of images does the poet use? Which senses are used?

_____

_____

7 Does the poem have an effective, striking, or climactic moment? Does it come to some kind of resolution?

_____

_____

8 What is the tone of the poem—solemn, playful, irreverent, mournful, objective? What is the poet trying to convey?

_____

_____

9 Note words that are used in an archaic, special, or unusual way.

_____

_____

✳ Choose one of the prompts below or create your own topic related to Dickinson's poems. Use your own paper for this assignment.

Topic 1: Write a comparison of the two poems, using the notes you made to answer the nine questions above. Use lines from the poems in your comparison.

Topic 2: Write a personal response to one of the two poems. State your understanding of the meaning of the poem, then show how you can apply it to an experience in your own life.

> A comparison of two poems may lead to greater understanding of both.

Assessing Your Strengths

Q What happens when a princess kisses a frog?

A The frog croaks. No, no, that's not right. The frog turns into a prince. And the prince and the princess live happily ever after.

That's one version! In this unit, you'll read not only the "happily ever after" version, but you'll read some of the contemporary versions, too. First, just in case you have forgotten the story, we'll give you the classic Brothers Grimm version. It does have its grim elements, too, as you will see. "The Frog Prince," in several different versions, is the basis for this midway reading and writing opportunity to show your strengths.

31 INTERACTING WITH THE TEXT

Some of you will remember the story of "The Frog Prince," while others in the class may not know it. Before talking about what you remember, jot down as much of the story as you know. Try to include any details that you may remember about it. If you don't remember ever hearing or reading the story, jot down any references with which you are familiar that include the idea of "kissing a frog" or a frog turning into a prince.

_____

_____

_____

_____

_____

_____

_____

_____

INTERACT WITH THE TEXT

This is one of the earliest versions, the most famous of the Grimm brothers' retellings of this tale. In the Response Notes, mark parts of the story that are familiar and parts that are surprising. You may wish to use two different colored pencils.

The Frog Prince as told by Jacob Ludwig Grimm and Wilhelm Carl Grimm

Response Notes

Once upon a time there was a king who had three daughters. In his courtyard there was a well with wonderful clear water. One hot summer day the oldest daughter went down and drew herself a glassful, but when she held it to the sun, she saw that it was cloudy. This seemed strange to her, and she was about to pour it back when a frog appeared in the water, stuck his head into the air, then jumped out onto the well's edge, saying:

If you will be my sweetheart dear,
Then I will give you water clear.

"Ugh! Who wants to be the sweetheart of an ugly frog!" exclaimed the princess and ran away. She told her sisters about the amazing frog down at the well who was making the water cloudy. The second one was curious, so she too went down and drew herself a glassful, but it was so cloudy that she could not drink it. Once again the frog appeared at the well's edge and said:

> If you will be my sweetheart dear,
> Then I will give you water clear.

"Not I!" said the princess, and ran away. Finally the third sister came and drew a glassful, but it was no better than before. The frog also said to her:

> If you will be my sweetheart dear,
> Then I will give you water clear.

"Why not! I'll be your sweetheart. Just give me some clean water," she said, while thinking, "There's no harm in this. You can promise him anything, for a stupid frog can never be your sweetheart."

The frog sprang back into the water, and when she drew another glassful it was so clear that the sun glistened in it with joy. She drank all she wanted and then took some up to her sisters, saying, "Why were you so stupid as to be afraid of a frog?"

The princess did not think anything more about it until that evening after she had gone to bed. Before she fell asleep she heard something scratching at the door and a voice singing:

> Open up! Open up!
> Youngest daughter of the king.
> Remember that you promised me
> While I was sitting in the well,
> That you would be my sweetheart dear,
> If I would give you water clear.

"Ugh! That's my boyfriend the frog," said the princess. "I promised, so I will have to open the door for him." She got up, opened the door a crack, and went back to bed. The frog hopped after her, then hopped onto her bed where he lay at her feet until the night was over and the morning dawned. Then he jumped down and disappeared out the door.

The next evening, when the princess once more had just gone to bed, he scratched and sang again at the door. The princess let him in, and he again lay at her feet until daylight came. He came again on the third evening, as on the two previous ones. "This is the last time that I'll let you in," said the princess. "It will not happen again in the future."

The king's daughter began to cry, for she was afraid of the cold frog which she did not like to touch, and which was now to sleep in her pretty, clean little bed. When she was in bed he crept to her and said, "I am tired, I want to sleep as well as you, lift me up or I will tell your father." At this she was terribly

angry, and took him up and threw him with all her might against the wall. "Now, will you be quiet, odious frog," said she. But when he fell down he was no frog but a king's son with kind and beautiful eyes.

He told her that he had been an enchanted frog and that she had broken the spell by promising to be his sweetheart. Then they both went to the king who gave them his blessing, and they were married. The two other sisters were angry with themselves that they had not taken the frog for their sweetheart. ❖

✳ Answer the questions below with a few notes. Use the notes to discuss the story with several classmates.

■ What do you think about the violent act of the princess?

_____

_____

■ What stereotypes do you find in the story?

_____

_____

■ If fairy tales were intended to teach children about the values of their society, what might those values be in "The Frog Prince"?

_____

_____

Fairy tales embody the values and customs of earlier societies while dealing with issues that remain important to us today.

■ "The Frog Prince" is one of many transformation stories. What about the nature of frogs makes the frog a particularly good choice for a "transformation story"?

_____

_____

Fairy tales just don't stay the same way. Every writer who reads one seems to want to write his or her own version. "The Frog Prince" has led to an amazing number of spin-offs.

One way writers deal with fairy tales is to give them alternative endings. Read this writer's continuation of "The Frog Prince." As you read, make notes in the **Response Notes** column whenever you find a connection to another fairy tale.

The Frog Prince Continued: A Story
by Jon Scieszka

Response Notes

The Princess kissed the frog. He turned into a prince. And they lived happily ever after... Well let's just say they lived sort of happily for a long time. Okay, so they weren't so happy. In fact, they were miserable.

"Stop sticking your tongue out like that," nagged the Princess. "How come you never want to go down to the pond anymore?" whined the Prince. The Prince and Princess were so unhappy. They didn't know what to do. "I would prefer that you not hop around on the furniture," said the Princess. "And it might be nice if you got out of the castle once in a while to slay a dragon or giant or whatever." The Prince didn't feel like going out and slaying anything. He just felt like running away. But then he reread his book. And it said right there at the end of his story: "They lived happily ever after. The End." So he stayed in the castle and drove the Princess crazy. Then one day, the Princess threw a perfectly awful fit. "First you keep me awake all night with your horrible, croaking snore. Now I find a lily pad in your pocket. I can't believe I actually kissed your slimy frog lips. Sometimes I think we would both be better off if you were still a frog." That's when the idea hit him. The Prince thought, "Still a frog. . . . Yes! That's it!"

And he ran off into the forest, looking for a witch who could turn him back into a frog. The Prince hadn't gone far when he ran into just the person he was looking for. "Miss Witch, Miss Witch. Excuse me, Miss Witch. I wonder if you could help me?" "Say, you're not looking for a princess to kiss are you?" asked the witch. "Oh, no. I've already been kissed. I'm the Frog Prince. Actually, I was hoping you could turn me back into a frog." "Are you sure you're not looking for a beautiful sleeping princess to kiss and wake up?" "No, no— I'm the Frog Prince." "That's funny. You don't look like a frog. Well, no matter. If you're a prince, you're a prince. And I'll have to cast a nasty spell on you. I can't have any princes waking up Sleeping Beauty before the hundred years are up."

Sleeping Beauty

The Prince didn't stick around to see which nasty spell the witch had in mind. He ran deeper into the forest until he came to a tiny cottage where he saw another lady who might help him. "Miss Witch, Miss Witch. Excuse me, Miss Witch. I wonder if you could help me. I'm a prince and—" "Eh? What did you say? Prince?" croaked the witch. "No. I mean, yes. I mean, no, I'm not the prince looking for Sleeping Beauty. But, yes, I'm the Frog Prince. And I'm looking for a member of your profession who can turn me back into a frog so I can live happily ever after." "Frog Prince, you say? That's funny. I thought frogs were little green guys with webbed feet. Well, no matter. If you're a prince, you're a prince. And I can't have any princes rescuing Snow White. Here—eat the rest of this apple."

The Prince, who knew his fairy tales (and knew a poisoned apple when he saw one), didn't even stay to say, "No, thank you." He turned and ran deeper into the forest. Soon he came to a strange-looking house with a witch outside. "Ahem. Miss Witch, Miss Witch. Excuse me, Miss Witch. I wonder if you could help me? I'm the Frog—" "If you're a frog, I'm the King of France," said the witch. "No, I'm not a frog. I'm the Frog Prince. But I need a witch to turn me back into a frog so I can live happily ever after can you do it?" said the Prince in one long breath. The witch eyed the Prince and licked her rather plump lips. "Why, of course, dearie. Come right in. Maybe I can fit you in for lunch." The Prince stopped on the slightly gummy steps. Something about this house seemed very familiar. He broke off a corner of the windowsill and tasted it. Gingerbread. "I hope you don't mind my asking, Miss Witch. But do you happen to know any children by the name of Hansel and Gretel?" "Why yes, Prince darling, I do. I'm expecting them for dinner."

The Prince, who, as we said before, knew his fairy tales, ran as fast as he could deeper into the forest. Soon he was completely lost. He saw someone standing next to a tree. The Prince walked up to her, hoping she wasn't a witch, for he'd quite had his fill of witches. "Madam. I am the Frog Prince. Could you help me?" "Gosh, do you need it," said the Fairy Godmother. "You are the worst-looking frog I've ever seen." "I am not a frog. I am the Frog Prince," said the Prince, getting a little annoyed. "And I need someone to turn me back

into a frog so I can live happily ever after." "Well, I'm on my way to see a girl in the village about going to a ball, but I suppose I could give it a try. I've never done frogs before, you know."

And with that the Fairy Godmother waved her magic wand, and turned the Prince into a beautiful . . . carriage. The Prince couldn't believe his rotten luck. The sun went down. The forest got spookier. And the Prince became more and more frightened. "Oh, what an idiot I've been. I could be sitting at home with the Princess, living happily ever after. But instead, I'm stuck here in the middle of this stupid forest, turned into a stupid carriage. Now I'll probably just rot and fall apart and live unhappily ever after." The Prince thought these terrible, frightening kinds of thoughts (and a few worse—too awful to tell), until far away in the village, the clock struck midnight.

The Carriage instantly turned back into his former Prince self, and ran by the light of the moon until he was safe inside his own castle. "Where have you been? I've been worried sick. You're seven hours late. Your dinner is cold. Your clothes are a mess."

The Prince looked at the Princess who had believed him when no one else in the world had, the Princess who actually kissed his slimy frog lips. The Princess who loved him. The Prince kissed the Princess. They both turned into frogs. And they hopped off happily ever after. The end. ❖

❋ Use your **Response Notes** to answer these questions.

■ Which other fairy tales are embedded in this story?

_____

_____

■ What do you think of the Prince's solution to his unhappiness?

_____

_____

■ What kind of person would write a story such as this?

_____

_____

FOCUS ON THE WRITER

Here's the answer to the last question on page 107. Read what Jon Scieszka (shown left) says about himself.

I read everything — comic books, newspapers, cereal boxes, poems — anything with writing on it. My favorite things to read are fairy tales, myths, and legends. When I'm not reading, I listen to music, watch cartoons, and sit in my chair and just think about stuff. I've always thought about being an author. One of the first books I read was *Green Eggs and Ham,* by Dr. Seuss. It made me realize that books could be goofy. It's the book that made *The Stinky Cheese Man* possible!

My ideas come from all different things: my kids, kids I've taught, kids I've learned from, watching movies, playing with my cat, talking to my wife, staring out the window, and about a million other places. But what turns the ideas into stories and books is sitting down and writing and re-writing and throwing away writing and writing some more. That's the hard part. I never know exactly how long it takes to write a story. I read a lot of stuff, think about different stories all the time, scribble things down on paper, type them up, change them, scribble again, think some more, add things....

I write books because I love to make kids laugh. I knew Lane Smith (illustrator of *The True Story of the Three Little Pigs!, The Stinky Cheese Man* and *Squids Will Be Squids*) would do a great job because we like a lot of the same cartoons and books and ideas. And we laugh at each other's bad jokes all of the time. Our audience is hardcore silly kids, and there are a lot of 'em out there! My motto in writing is: "Never underestimate the intelligence of your audience." Kids can be silly *and* smart!

Before I became an author, I attended military school, studied pre-med in college, and worked as a lifeguard and house painter. I also taught computers, math, science, and history to kids grades 1-8.

I now live in Brooklyn, N.Y., with my wife Jeri, daughter Casey and my son Jake. I like fruit and a cup of coffee for breakfast, but I usually steal some of Jake's Honey Nut Cheerios or his pancakes. If you'd like to call out my name, it's pronounced "SHEH-ska." It kind of rhymes with Fresca.

MAKE CONNECTIONS: WRITE YOUR OWN BIOGRAPHY

✳ If you grow up to be a writer, what sort of thing would you write? You might begin by thinking of what you like to read, like Jon Scieszka does in his biography. Imagine that you are grown up and have published something (you decide what). Now write your own biography of how you came to write the kind of thing you do (be specific here). Tell what kind of person you are, using Jon Scieszka's biography as an inspiration. You might even want to illustrate it with a comical self-portrait.

_____

_____

_____

_____

_____

_____

_____

_____

_____

_____

_____

_____

_____

_____

_____

_____

_____

_____

After you have finished, share your writing with your group or the whole class.

Writers are drawn to the possibilities of rewriting or continuing fairy tales, often in a humorous mode.

33 EXPLORE MULTIPLE PERSPECTIVES

Poets, as well as fiction writers, have been intrigued by "The Frog Prince." This is a version of the frog-and-prince story in a poem called "Annunciation" by Adrianne Marcus, who presents another perspective. It closely follows many of the elements of the Grimm brothers' story. It introduces new elements as well, and the last stanza may give you pause as you consider the question it asks.

In the **Response Notes** column, note your comments about elements that are the same as in the classic version and those that are different. It will help to color code the parts of the poem that refer to classic and new.

Response Notes

Annunciation by Adrianne Marcus

Disgusting, she thought, as she stroked
that damp green back, noted the fragile
front legs, the muscular thighs. Still, she
had given her word. After all it was her
favorite golden ball, and she had to have
it back He cocked his head, winsomely,
staring at her with bulbous eyes, and his
tongue flicked out, once, then twice.

Revolting, she thought, this stupid bargain
With a talking frog; and talk he did.
Reminded her constantly of promises
made, as he ate off her golden plate,
slept in her bed on the finest Egyptian
linens. By dawn, he was gone, and
she thought that was the end of it.

Unimaginable, she said, when he reappeared
that night, and the next, but by then
she was used to him, and found he could
discuss Wittgenstein, knew a bit of Homer
and offered to help her with her lessons.
By now, his skin felt soft beneath her hand,
his eyes a delicate mixture of hazel and gold,
his forked tongue intriguing.

Wittgenstein is a 20th century philosopher. Homer was a ninth century B.C. Greek writer.

Fate has a curious way of taking us at
our word, and sometimes the frog
metamorphoses into a handsome
prince and sometimes
he doesn't. Which would you pick?
Remember: the bargain is forever.

Use your **Response Notes** to compare which elements are the same
in both versions and which elements are new in Marcus's poem.

Elements in classic version	New elements

❋ Focus on the last stanza. What do you think Adrianne Marcus
means, especially in the last line? Is the bargain forever,
or isn't it?

_____

_____

Think about the versions of "The Frog Prince" you have read. Make
some notes about these statements:

■ Since the frog is an animal that "transforms" itself as it grows
from a tadpole to a frog, it is a natural for a story about transformation or adopting another persona.

■ The idea of transformation underlies a lot of fairy tales and
myths. In your group, think of some stories or myths you know
that involve transformations.

_____

_____

_____

_____

Writers get ideas from
looking at familiar stories from
a different perspective.

34

You have now had experience in using all of the essential strategies of reading and writing together in one unit. Using what you have learned in all of the units so far, we want you to demonstrate your best thinking in both reading and writing.

You have three choices for your writing assignment. Choose one. Think about the topic you will write about. What will be your main idea? What are your supporting details? Create a concept web below. Then write a draft of from one to three pages of regular notebook paper.

Choice 1: Think about how people feel free from their own limitations when wearing masks. Consider the positive and negative aspects of adopting another persona. Use examples from your own experience as well as from your reading when you write to this prompt. Refer to "The Frog Prince" in your paper.

Choice 2: Write about the idea of transformation in fairy tales, myths, or stories you have read or watched (television and movies are okay here). Refer to "The Frog Prince" in your paper.

Choice 3: Think about what you have read in this unit, the original classic version of "The Frog Prince" and adaptations. Now write your own adaptation. You may write a continuation, a poem, a story, or even a comic book version.

❊ Write the number of your choice here: _____

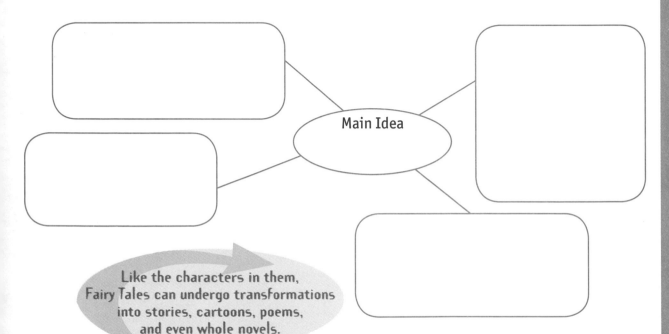

Main Idea

Like the characters in them, Fairy Tales can undergo transformations into stories, cartoons, poems, and even whole novels.

SHARING YOUR FIRST DRAFT WITH YOUR PARTNER OR GROUP

✳ Meet with a partner or a group to share the first draft of your paper. Before you read each other's papers, we think it is important for you to know what your teacher will look for when he or she reads your story.

An outstanding story will

✳ respond directly to one of the three prompts.

✳ show your understanding of the basic elements of "The Frog Prince."

✳ show how well you are able to

- organize your ideas
- write clear sentences that flow when read aloud
- make good word choices (specific nouns, vivid verbs)
- spell words correctly
- punctuate and capitalize correctly

✳ Read your paper aloud to a partner or members of a small group. When you read your paper, the other members should listen carefully. When each person finishes reading, the other members should tell the writer what they liked about the paper. Then they should use the items in the box to help the reader improve.

✳ As your group talks about your paper, make notes so that when you revise it, you will remember what they suggested.

MAKING A FINAL COPY

✳ Using the suggestions of your group, make the revisions you think will improve your paper. Then make a clean copy of your final draft. Remember to give it a title.

REFLECTION

It is important to stop periodically and reflect on what you are learning. Then you can evaluate where you need to go from here. Fill in the chart. Then write about how you have improved as a reader and writer.

Essential Strategies of Reading and Writing	How I rate myself at the beginning of the *Daybook*		How I rate myself now	
	5=High, 1=Low	Comments	5=High, 1=Low	Comments
Example: Interacting with the text	2	I didn't know how to annotate or ask questions.	4	I'm pretty good at it now.
Interacting with the text				
Making connections				
Exploring multiple perspectives				
Focusing on language and craft				
Studying an author				

_____

_____

_____

_____

_____

_____

_____

_____

Reflecting is an important part of learning how to strengthen your reading and writing skills.

Expanding Your Repertoire

What does the saying "We are what we eat" say about you? Are you natural and fresh, like a just-picked apple or a vine-ripened tomato? Or are you, like many Americans, more of a greasy, fast-food burger or a sweet rainbow-colored cereal? In this age of food that comes pre-sliced, pre-cooked, preserved, and packaged, the idea of eating more naturally may seem strange.

In this unit you enter a laboratory that makes french fries taste the way they do, and you will go to an "edible schoolyard," where kids grow and prepare their own food. You'll also meet two women who have devoted their lives to spreading the word about natural, delicious food.

As we discussed in the first unit in this *Daybook,* being a strong reader requires that you build a reading **repertoire**— a set of skills and strategies—to use with all the different kinds of texts you encounter. In this unit you will work on **expanding your repertoire** as you build on what you've practiced in previous lessons.

When you read, what goes on in your head? If you're really engaged with what you're reading, there is a whole lot going on in there. You are **interacting with the text.** Being aware of what goes on in your head is called *metacognitive awareness. Metacognitive* means "thinking about what's going on in your mind."

Think about the ways you interact with texts that really engage you. Some common ways to interact with texts are these:

- Take notes, highlight, or circle words or phrases.
- Visualize, or picture, what is going on.
- Ask questions or wonder about things you read.
- "Talk back" to the author or characters.
- Pause to think or gather information from a dictionary or another person.

Even if you are a very strong reader, you may find some texts challenging. It could be that you are distracted and have something else on your mind. It could be that the topic is new, complex, or not particularly interesting to you. Or it could be that the writing is challenging, using sophisticated words and complicated sentences. A good way to tackle a challenging text is to practice *metacognitive awareness* and to interact with it as much as possible.

The selection below is an excerpt from a nonfiction book about the author's investigation of the fast food industry. As you read it, practice *metacognitive awareness.* In the **Response Notes** column, record what you are thinking about as you read.

from **Fast Food Nation** by Eric Schlosser

Response Notes

Bud Mandeville, the plant manager, led me up a narrow, wooden staircase inside one of the plant's storage buildings. On the top floor, the staircase led to a catwalk, and beneath my feet I saw a mound of potatoes that was twenty feet deep and a hundred feet wide and almost as long as two football fields. The building was cool and dark, kept year-round at a steady 46 degrees. In the dim light the potatoes looked like grains of sand on a beach. This was one of seven storage buildings on the property.

Outside, tractor-trailers arrived from the fields, carrying potatoes that had just been harvested. The trucks dumped their loads onto spinning rods that brought the larger potatoes into the building and let the small potatoes, dirt, and rocks fall to the ground. The rods led to a rock trap, a tank of water in which the potatoes floated and the rocks sank to the bottom. The plant used water systems to float potatoes gently this way and that way, guiding different sizes out of different holding bays, then flushing them into a three-foot-deep stream that ran beneath the cement floor. The interior of the processing plant was gray, massive, and well-lit, with huge pipes running along the walks, steel catwalks, workers in hardhats, and plenty of loud machinery. If there weren't potatoes bobbing and floating past, you might think the place was an oil refinery.

Conveyer belts took the wet, clean potatoes into a machine that blasted them with steam for twelve seconds, boiled the water under their skins, and exploded their skins off. Then the potatoes were pumped into a preheat tank and shot through a Lamb Water Gun Knife. They emerged as shoestring fries. Four video cameras scrutinized them from different angles, looking for flaws. When a french fry with a blemish was detected, an optical sorting machine time-sequenced a single burst of compressed air that knocked the bad fry off the production line and onto a separate conveyer belt, which carried it to a machine with tiny automated knives that precisely removed the blemish. And then the fry was returned to the main production line.

Sprays of hot water blanched the fries, gusts of hot air dried them, and 25,000 pounds of boiling oil friend them to a slight crisp. Air cooled by compressed ammonia gas quickly froze them, a computerized sorter divided them into six-pound batches, and a device that spun like an out-of-control lazy Susan used centrifugal force to align the french fries so that they all pointed in the same directions. The fries were sealed in brown bags, then the bags were loaded by robots into cardboard boxes, and the boxes were stacked by robots onto wooden pallets. Forklifts driven by human beings took the pallets to a freezer for storage. Inside that freezer I saw 20 million pounds of french fries. . . . ❖

✳ Take a moment to think about what went on in your head as you read, and add comments to your **Response Notes.**

It is always nice to be able to make sense of everything we read. In reality, though, we better understand some texts and find them more meaningful than others. How hard you work to understand details depends on your purpose for reading. Sometimes, it may be enough to just determine the main point of each paragraph. Other times, every little detail matters.

✳ Imagine that you read the selection above because your friend told you it was interesting. And, you love french fries, so you're curious what it says. In that case, you might decide to read just for the main point of each paragraph. If you missed some details here and there, it would not matter. In the space that follows, explain the main idea of each paragraph.

Paragraph 1: _____

Paragraph 2: _____

Paragraph 3: _____

Paragraph 4: _____

✳ Now imagine that you read the selection because you are writing an article on fast food for your school newspaper. It's important that you get your facts straight. Summarize, in detail and in your own words, what you read.

_____

_____

_____

_____

_____

_____

_____

_____

_____

_____

_____

_____

> Using metacognitive awareness helps you to interact with and understand challenging texts.

In this lesson, you will practice **making connections** with another piece of nonfiction. You might make connections to yourself, to other things you have read, to other things you have learned or know about, or even to the selection in the previous lesson.

In *Fast Food Nation,* Eric Schlosser explains that most processed food is made so that it can be kept and transported easily, such as by picking vegetables or fruits that are not yet ripe or by freezing or dehydrating food. These processes often make the food tasteless. To make up for this, food processing companies such as fast food restaurant chains hire scientists to create flavors that enhance the taste of the food. In the following excerpt, Schlosser visits one of the "flavor labs" in which these flavors are created. A flavorist (a scientist who creates the artificial and "natural" flavors) lets Schlosser smell some of the aromas he has created.

While you read, practice *metacognitive awareness.* Remember to read slowly, pause when you need to, and reread any parts that are unclear. Ask yourself, what do I already know about this topic or these words? What does this remind me of? When you make a connection, write it in the **Response Notes** column.

from **Fast Food Nation** by Eric Schlosser

Response Notes

...The flavor industry is highly secretive. Its leading companies will not divulge the precise formulas or flavor compounds or the identities of clients. The secrecy is deemed essential for protecting the reputation of beloved brands. The fast food chains, understandably, would like the public to believe that the flavors of their food somehow originate in their restaurant kitchens, not in distant factories run by other firms.

...Grainger [a flavorist] had brought a dozen small glass bottles from the lab. After he opened each bottle, I dipped a fragrance testing filter into it. The filters were long white strips of paper designed to absorb aroma chemicals without producing off-notes. Before placing the strips of paper before my nose, I closed my eyes. Then I inhaled deeply, and one food after another was conjured from the glass bottles. I smelled fresh cherries, black olives, sautéed onions, and shrimp. Grainger's most remarkable creation took me by surprise. After closing my eyes, I suddenly smelled a grilled hamburger. The aroma was uncanny, almost miraculous. It smelled like someone in the room was flipping burgers on a hot grill. But when I opened my eyes, there was just a narrow strip of white paper and a smiling flavorist. ❖

✳ Compare your **Response Notes** with those of a partner. Were your connections similar? Discuss them.

✳ How do your connections help you to understand the text better?

_____

_____

_____

_____

✳ How would you describe the main idea of the excerpts you have read from *Fast Food Nation*? In other words, what do you think is the main point, or the key idea, Eric Schlosser is trying to share with you?

_____

_____

_____

_____

_____

Share your response with your partner. Did you have similar ideas? Discuss why each of you chose the main idea you did.

✳ To make a connection with your own life, consider how what you read could influence your consumption of fast food. Use the space below to list ideas for a personal essay on how you feel about eating fast food. Remember that the beginning of the essay should state your main idea. The middle should expand the idea and present examples and details. The end should restate the focus and make a final statement.

Main idea: _____

_____

Details: _____

_____

_____

Final idea: _____

Title
_____

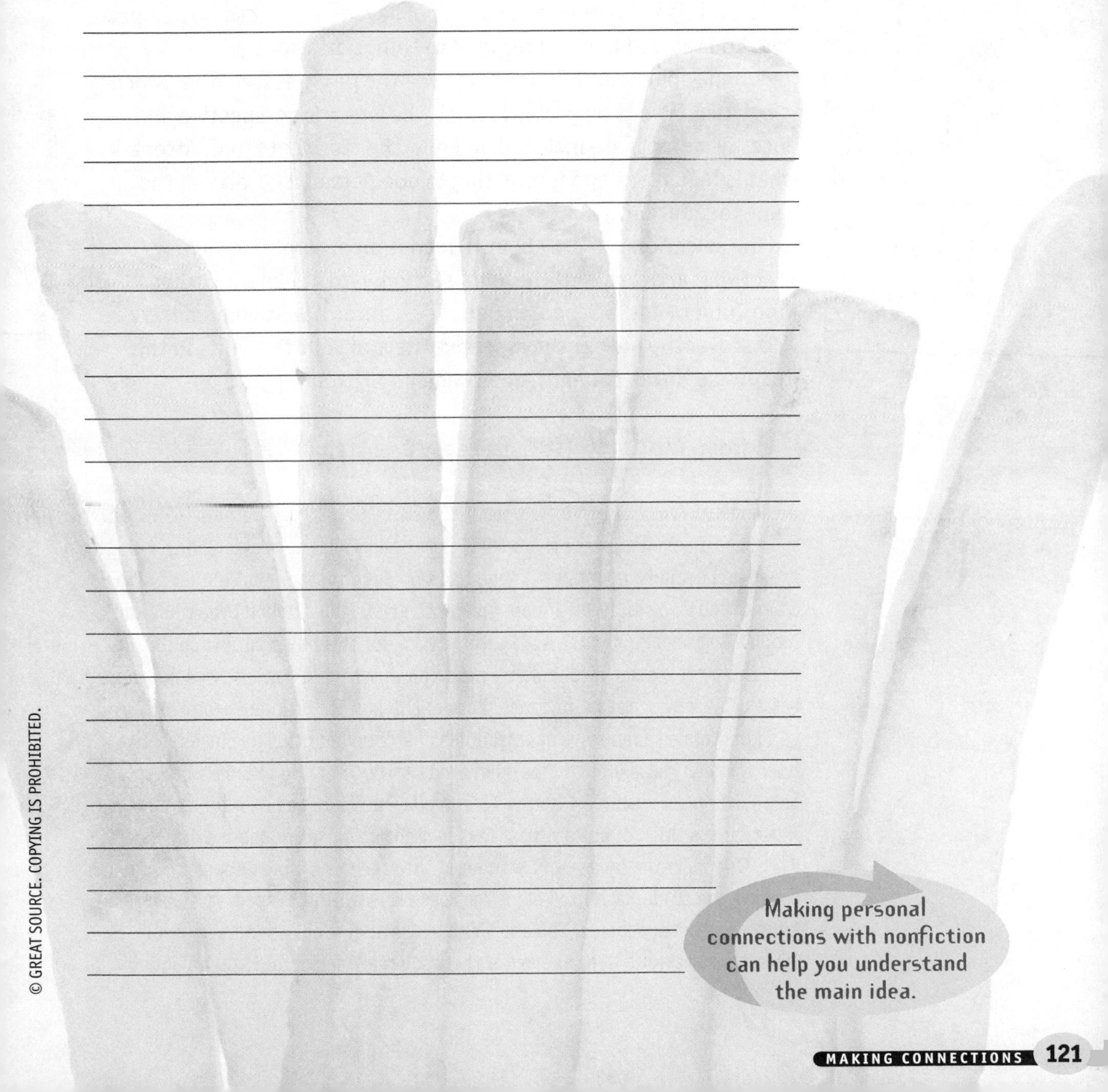

_____

_____

_____

_____

_____

_____

_____

_____

_____

_____

_____

_____

_____

_____

_____

_____

_____

_____

_____

_____

_____

Making personal connections with nonfiction can help you understand the main idea.

Imagine that you accompany a newspaper reporter on a visit to a middle school in Berkeley, California. The school is famous for its schoolyard, which has been turned into a garden that is cared for by students as part of their schoolwork. A famous restaurant owner, Alice Waters, started the project. You plan to write an article about it for your school newspaper, and the other reporter, Peggy Orenstein, is writing an article for the *New York Times.* Even though you are writing about the same topic, you and Ms. Orenstein will write different articles. This is because no two people have the exact same perspective. You see and feel and respond to things differently.

When you read nonfiction, examine the **perspective** from which it is written. Even though it is factual, the writer's perspective influences what facts are included and how the story gets told. After all, what is important and interesting to one person isn't always the same for another.

The selection you are about to read is an excerpt from a *New York Times* article about the Edible Schoolyard at Martin Luther King Junior Middle School in Berkeley, California. As you read, try to discover the author's perspective. Record your thoughts in the **Response Notes** column. An example is written for you.

from "**Food Fighter**" by Peggy Orenstein

Response Notes

It sounds like the author thinks the kids eat really badly!

As students from King whirled around, flirting, playing basketball, lolling on the grass, I asked a few of them what they had eaten the previous day. A sixth-grade girl could recall only that she had two doughnuts for breakfast and half a sandwich and candy for lunch. An eighth-grade girl skipped breakfast and lunch altogether and had a soda after school, followed by a sandwich for dinner. The boys ate more consistently, but the nutritional content was not much better. Burgers or pizza for lunch. Lots of chicken for dinner. Vegetables beyond carrots or corn were scarce, unless ketchup counts. The closest thing to fruit for many was a bag of fruit-flavored candy. Only two children had eaten balanced meals within 24 hours. This in a town renowned as a foodie's mecca. Nationally, a third of children eat fast food for at least one meal a day.

... One morning last year, I wandered through the Edible Schoolyard garden reading the student-painted signs for roses, spearmint, grapes, strawberries, fig trees, onions, poppies. The sixth and seventh graders spend 10 weekly 90-minute sessions here as part of their science curriculum and an equal amount of time in the kitchen with their humanities classes. The eighth graders visit each venue about six times a year.

Kelsey Siegel, who works as garden manager, listed the tasks of the day: the students could choose to help build a bench using a sustainable cement mixture of clay and straw. Or they could plant mustard greens or radish seedlings. Or weed the garlic. As a special treat, they also got to make pizza in an outdoor wood-burning stone oven, built by a friend of [restaurateur Alice] Waters's.

Within a few minutes, the students had scattered. By the pizza oven one group rolled out a cornmeal crust, brushed it with a layer of garlic-infused olive oil and sprinkled the top with feta cheese, spring onions, chard, rosemary and mint. "This cheese smells like feet!" announced a compact boy in a red fleece pullover. Then, realizing he'd been impolitic, he added, "I guess it's a good way to eat if you want to be organic and vegetarian."

As I walked back to the kitchen, I bumped into Waters and [Edible Schoolyard program coordinator Marsha] Guerrero. "What did they think of the pizza?" Waters asked expectantly. Before I could reply, Guerrero, the voice of pragmatism, jumped in. "They hated the cheese, didn't they?" Waters furrowed her brow a moment, then brightened. "If the kids think feta is weird, why not have them make their own fresh mozzarella? It's the easiest thing in the world."

…Waters is onto something: teaching about new foods, emphasizing participation and offering choices are all critical to nudging children toward better diets. ❖

✳ How does the author seem to feel about the Edible Schoolyard project?

_____

_____

_____

_____

_____

✳ What evidence from the story suggests that is her perspective?

_____

_____

_____

_____

_____

✳ Consider the boy who said, "This cheese smells like feet!" and "I guess it's a good way to eat if you want to be organic and vegetarian." What do these quotes suggest about his perspective?

_____

_____

_____

_____

✳ Now write an article about the Edible Schoolyard from the boy's perspective.

_____

_____

_____

_____

_____

_____

_____

_____

_____

_____

_____

_____

_____

_____

_____

_____

_____

_____

_____

Examine multiple perspectives to better understand all sides of nonfiction text.

When you imagine studying the **language and craft** of a piece of writing, you probably imagine reading fiction or poetry. The phrase suggests an author *crafting* a great work of literature. Great writing can be found in any genre, however, including nonfiction. Similar to fiction, engaging nonfiction is written with style. All authors have their own style, but they might use similar techniques:

- Ask questions for the reader to think about.
- Choose quotes that are interesting or dramatic.
- Use repetition for emphasis.
- Use words that convey and stir emotions.
- Use descriptive words that help readers develop a mental picture.
- Vary sentence length to keep a reader's interest.
- Write very short sentences to make clear points.
- Use incomplete sentences for impact.

The author of the selection you are about to read is Ruth Reichl (pronounced *RYE-shul*), who became famous for writing about food. The selection is a profile of Alice Waters (at right), the restaurant owner and food activist who started the Edible Schoolyard. Review the techniques listed above. As you read, pay attention to Reichl's writing style. Take notes about language and craft in the **Response Notes** column.

Alice Waters by Ruth Reichl

Alice Waters lies in bed at night worrying about what to feed you. She knows that she can make you happy. She also knows, in her hidden heart, that if she can find the perfect dish to feed each person who comes to her door, she can change the world.

Every great cook secretly believes in the power of food. Alice Waters just believes this more than anybody else. She is certain that we are what we eat, and she has made it her mission in life to make sure that people eat beautifully. Waters is creating a food revolution, even if she has to do it one meal at a time.

Alice didn't set out to change the way America eats. She just wanted to feed her friends. Having been to France, she had seen the way a good bistro could become the heart of a neighborhood, a place where people went for comfort and sustenance. She was not a professional cook, but she enjoyed feeding

Reichl writes smooth and varied sentences.

Response Notes

people, and she envisioned a cozy little café, which would be open every day for breakfast, lunch, and dinner, a place where everyone from the dishwashers to the cooks would be well-paid, a sort of endless party where everyone would have fun. Reality soon set in. Faced with financial ruin, Chez Panisse was forced to become a real business. Still, the dream did not die. It just changed.

"I was more obsessed," Alice explains. If she was going to have a restaurant, it was going to be the very best one she could possibly manage. Even if that meant rethinking the whole concept of what a restaurant might be.

She began with the ingredients. Every chef dreams of great produce, but most make do with what is available in the market. Not Alice. Disgusted with the fish that was sold in stores, she bought a truck and sent someone down to the port to find fishermen as they docked their boats. When she could not find the baby lettuces she had loved in France, she tore up her backyard and grew her own. She found foragers to hunt for mushrooms. She persuaded farmers to let their lambs run wild through the hills. She demanded better bread. Before long, she had developed an entire network of people producing food just for her.

※ Pause for a moment and review your **Response Notes**.
Compare notes with a partner and discuss Ruth Reichl's style.
Then continue reading and taking notes.

The results were electric. Chez Panisse served only one meal a day, but people reserved months ahead of time and took their chances. You would find them shaking their heads over the menu, wailing, "Chicken? I've come all the way from Maine for chicken?" Then the dish would arrive, and they'd look down with dismay and say, "It's just a piece of chicken," as if they had somehow expected the poor bird to turn into a swan as it cooked. But they'd waited months for the reservation, so they would take a bite of the chicken and a sort of wonder would come over their faces. "It's the best chicken I have ever tasted," they'd whisper reverently. "I never knew that food could taste so good."

And Alice, walking by, would smile her secret little smile. Because once again, she had done it. She had given them food that they would remember, a taste that would linger long beyond that night. And they would know, ever after, how a chicken raised in the open air, fed on corn, and cooked with care, could taste.

She knew that they would carry that flavor away with them, and that every time they ate a chicken, no matter where it might be, they would remember.

And if Alice had her way, they would go looking for that chicken—or that tomato, or that strawberry—until they found it. Because she had given them more than a meal—she had given them a memory.

There is only one Chez Panisse. In this age of multiple restaurants, the restaurant has no clones in London, Las Vegas, or Tokyo. Because Alice Waters

has more than money on her mind. And she has now turned her attention to the next generation. Her latest project? Feeding the children. She wants every school in America to have a garden and every child to have an opportunity to discover the taste of fresh food.

Her fight goes on. Her revolution continues. She knows that all it takes is one taste. It just has to be the right one. ❖

✳ Use your **Response Notes** to fill in the Language and Craft Chart below. An example is done for you.

A stylistic technique Ruth Reichl uses	An example of this technique	The effect of this technique
Uses emotion words	Alice Waters lies in bed at night **worrying** about what to feed you. She knows that she can make you **happy.**	It makes me interested in the writing right away. I feel emotional, too. I feel like I personally know Alice right away, since I can feel what she feels.

Nonfiction authors use writing techniques that convey their own personal styles.

40

STUDYING AN AUTHOR

Ruth Reichl is one of the most widely respected and influential food writers of our time. Learning about her life and perspective can help us to understand how she became the writer she is today.

The selection that follows is from an interview with Reichl. As you read it, write **Response Notes** as a way to highlight important or interesting facts you learn. After you have read, you will use your notes to write a speech about Reichl.

from "**A Taste for Life**" by Jeffrey L. Perlah

Response Notes

[While her memoir] *Tender at the Bone* is a celebration of food, Reichl notes that "food has always meant more to me than just eating and recipes. It's about people. And I wanted this book to be about people."

Q **Early on, you discovered that "food could be a way of making sense of the world."**

A "It's a way of giving yourself something of quality. Just to make yourself a perfect egg in the morning is a way of saying, 'I respect myself.'"

Q **The book points out that sweets are a big part of the beginner's repertoire.**

A "You learn very early that dessert is sort of a cheap trick. As a beginning cook, you make cookies and brownies, and other sweets, and people love them even if they're not great."

Q **What's challenging about being a restaurant critic in New York City?**

A "When Craig Claiborne [formerly of the *New York Times*] was doing restaurant criticism, he had to know about French food, continental food, maybe a little bit about Italian food, and that was pretty much it. Today, you have to know about food from all over the world, and, if you don't, you have to learn about it. No credible critic today can talk about Japanese food without really having some knowledge of it. It's more so in New York than in many other places."

Q **Your college friend Mac first made you aware of the way food was bringing people together, and keeping them apart.**

A "A lot of foods eaten by Europeans are considered disgusting by Americans. If you go to any restaurant in France, you're likely to find kidneys, livers, and brains. And eating a lot of garlic was something that ostracized Jews and Italians from polite society in New York. If you showed up with garlic on your breath, it often classified you as lower class. But one of the great things that has happened today is we eat foods from many different cultures. Food doesn't keep us apart now."

Q **Was your mother's lack of good cooking skills a factor in your approach to food?**

A "It was not so much her cooking skills as the fact that she was taste blind. She would leave butter uncovered in the refrigerator, put it on the table, and later in the day I would say, 'I can't eat it.' And she would taste it and say, 'there's nothing wrong with it.' I would taste things that she couldn't."

Q **On the other hand, your father was a book designer. Was that an influence on your writing?**

A "I think so. I was brought up in a world of books. My parents never had a television. Books were really their whole life. And certainly words were. I think I grew up really feeling the importance of telling stories, making a reality out of these little black marks on a paper. I was an only child, and my way of making a world for myself was through reading." ✦

✳ Based on what you read and the **Response Notes** you wrote, what can you infer about Ruth Reichl's personality?

_____

_____

_____

✳ Imagine that you are at an awards dinner for influential writers. You have been asked to introduce Ruth Reichl. Your research has turned up the following details about Ruth Reichl's life:

- Began writing about food in 1972 when she published *Mmmmm: A Feastiary*
- Involved with writing or editing more than 25 books, including three memoirs and numerous cookbooks
- Was chef and co-owner of The Swallow Restaurant in Berkeley, California
- Has been the restaurant critic for *New West* magazine, *California* magazine, the *Los Angeles Times*, and *The New York Times*
- Received the James Beard Award for restaurant criticism and for journalism

On the next page write the speech you would give to introduce Ruth Reichl, using language and craft in a style that is your own. Be sure to include facts about her life and work, as well as comments about her writing.

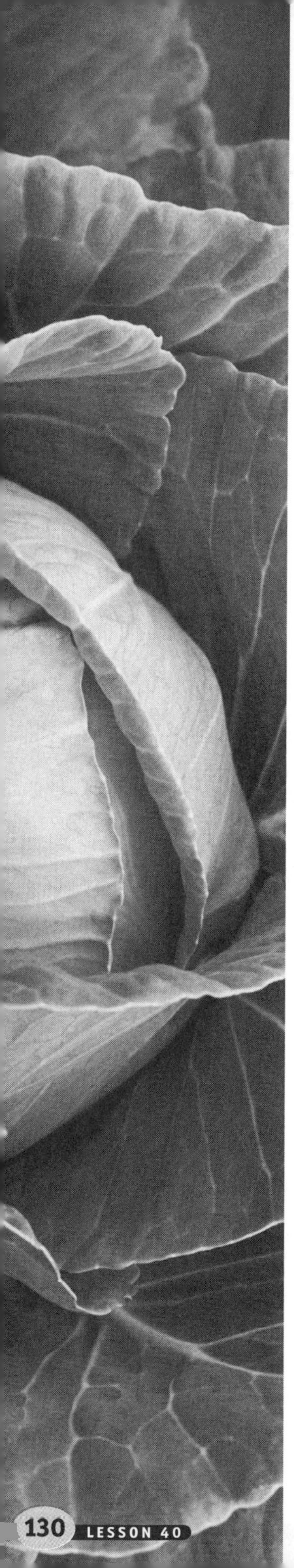

Title
_____

_____

_____

_____

_____

_____

_____

_____

_____

_____

_____

_____

_____

_____

_____

_____

_____

_____

_____

_____

_____

_____

※ With a partner, practice performing your speech. Compare the differences in your personal styles, as well as different facts and ideas you chose to include.

Writers' lives influence their ideas and styles of writing.

Interacting with the Text

Skim the pages in this lesson. You might be surprised. Pictures that look like comics? Why would a book about critical reading and writing include excerpts from a graphic novel?

More and more of our information comes from **visual images.** We find them all around us—on television, in movies, in advertisements, and elsewhere. Visual images convey information, attitudes, and biases, just as print texts do. They entertain, persuade, and inform. Yet, if we do not learn to read them carefully, we may unconsciously and uncritically just absorb the messages. That would be dangerous. Critical readers and writers need to pay attention not only to words but also to meanings and messages. They need to question and evaluate. Knowing how words and pictures work together to communicate messages will help you better understand and question the content. Many of the strategies you have used to interact with print text will help you with visual texts.

If you think that comic art presents only entertaining stories about superheroes, you will be surprised. The lessons in this unit focus on one of the most devastating and tragic events in history—the Holocaust.

41 MAKING INFERENCES

Active readers understand what they read by making reasonable guesses, or inferring. When you infer, you combine what you already know with the information provided in the text. Read the following first-person account from a young man who was a teenager during Hitler's rise to power in Germany. What **inference** can you make about his family background?

from **Parallel Journeys** by Eleanor Ayer with Helen Waterford and Alfons Heck

Unlike our elders, we children of the 1930's had never known a Germany without Nazis. From our very first year in the *Volksschule* or elementary school, we received daily doses of Nazisms. These we swallowed as naturally as our morning milk. Never did we question what our teachers said. We simply believed whatever was crammed into us. And never for a moment did we doubt how fortunate we were to live in a country with such a promising future. ❖

✳ Write your inference and the reason for it here. What background knowledge did you combine with clues from the paragraph?

_____

_____

_____

_____

When you read a visual text, you draw inferences from the visual and textual material the author provides. Making inferences about the characters helps you better understand who they are and their relationships to other characters. In *Maus: A Survivor's Tale,* Art Spiegelman tells the story of his father, a Jewish survivor of the Holocaust. Although it is a true story, Spiegelman has chosen to draw all of the characters with animal heads and human bodies. In the excerpt on the following page, Vladek, Spiegelman's father, has been released from a prison camp but ends up in the wrong part of Poland. To return to his town of Sosnowiec requires a dangerous journey. What inferences can you make about the characters' relationships in this excerpt?

✳ Use the Inference Chart to record your conclusions about the characters. In the third column tell what characteristics and relationships are suggested by the animals Spiegelman uses.

INFERENCE CHART

Animal	Human	Characteristics and Relationships
Pig	Polish train conductor	
Cat	German official	
Mouse	Jew	Mice are small animals who do not have power over larger animals. They are chased and killed by cats. Vladek disguised himself in Poland by putting on a pig nose so that he would look like a Pole.

Making inferences from the words, the pictures, and your background knowledge helps you better understand the text.

When you are reading, how can you tell what is important so that you can pay particular attention to it? You probably know that a textbook gives clues to important information by using headings and bold print. In fiction, the author might use symbols or repetition to give ideas added weight. Artists also use a variety of techniques to tell you what's important.

In the following excerpt from *Maus,* Vladek tells his son Art about the trip that Vladek and his wife Anja made before the war. The birth of their first son, Art's brother, had resulted in Anja's having a nervous breakdown. The doctor prescribed a stay in a sanitarium in Czechoslovakia where she could regain her health.

from Maus: A Survivor's Tale by Art Spiegelman

✳ The visuals for this part of the story contain a lot of information. In the box below, quickly write everything you noticed.

```

```

Use visual and textual clues to identify what is important in a text.

✳ Share what you noticed with a partner. Together, decide what was most important and circle those items. Write an explanation of how you knew one of the items was important.

_____

_____

What makes your favorite writers stand out? You might say it's the way they write the stories they tell. It's how they put words together and the details they include. These are elements of their **style.** Yet, they generally observe the conventions of whatever they are writing. Conventions are the elements that make a science fiction story different from a mystery story. If a story is set in the future, for example, and includes aspects of science such as robots or unusual plants, you expect that it will be science fiction.

Authors of graphic novels work the same way. They observe the conventions of the genre of graphic novels into which they infuse their own individual style. Comic artists use a variety of conventions to show passage of time, to emphasize ideas, and to differentiate between narration and dialogue. Read the following excerpt from *Maus.* This scene is a continuation of the one you read in Lesson 42. Vladek, Anja, and others are on a train on their way to the sanitarium in Czechoslovakia.

from **Maus: A Survivor's Tale** by Art Spiegelman

✳ Looking at the excerpts in Lesson 42 and in this lesson, find and label one example of each element of craft. Use the following labels: **T** for time, **E** for emphasis, **N** for narration, and **D** for dialogue. Compare your findings with a partner or a small group. Record your findings in the boxes.

Time	**E**mphasis
Narration	**D**ialogue

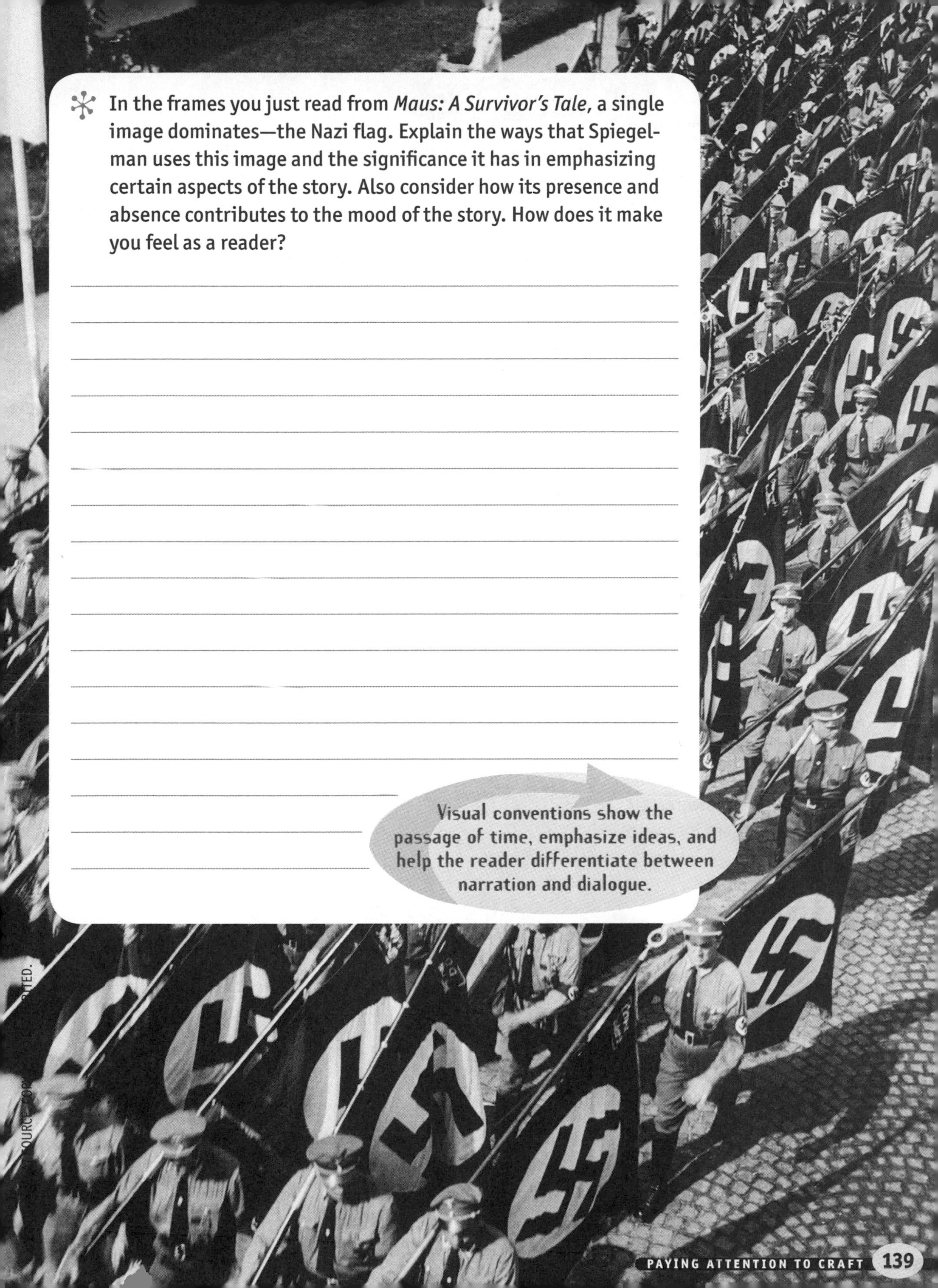

✳ In the frames you just read from *Maus: A Survivor's Tale*, a single image dominates—the Nazi flag. Explain the ways that Spiegelman uses this image and the significance it has in emphasizing certain aspects of the story. Also consider how its presence and absence contributes to the mood of the story. How does it make you feel as a reader?

_____

_____

_____

_____

_____

_____

_____

_____

_____

_____

_____

Visual conventions show the passage of time, emphasize ideas, and help the reader differentiate between narration and dialogue.

44

Proficient readers ask **questions.** They use their questions to **clarify** meaning or to learn more about something that interests them. They also ask questions to better understand how the author has created and presented a story. In Lesson 41 you probably had to ask yourself a question before you made an inference about why the Jews are portrayed as mice in *Maus*. To answer that question, you called on your background knowledge of the characteristics of certain animals. Some questions, though, are answered directly in the text. Answering other questions sometimes requires referring to another text.

Reread the sections of *Maus* in Lessons 41, 42, and 43. Then think of **questions** you could ask that would help someone else better understand this book. Write those questions in the boxes below.

Two questions that can be answered by referring directly to the text	*What nationality was the border guard when Vladek was trying to return to Sosnowiec?*
Two questions that can be answered by making an inference	
Two questions that can be answered by referring to another text	*What is a pogrom?*

✳ Discuss with a partner or small group two questions that interest you. Write a summary of your discussion below and explain how asking questions helped you understand the story.

_____

_____

_____

_____

_____

_____

_____

_____

_____

_____

_____

_____

_____

_____

_____

_____

_____

_____

_____

_____

_____

_____

_____

Ask questions about what you read if you want to understand it better.

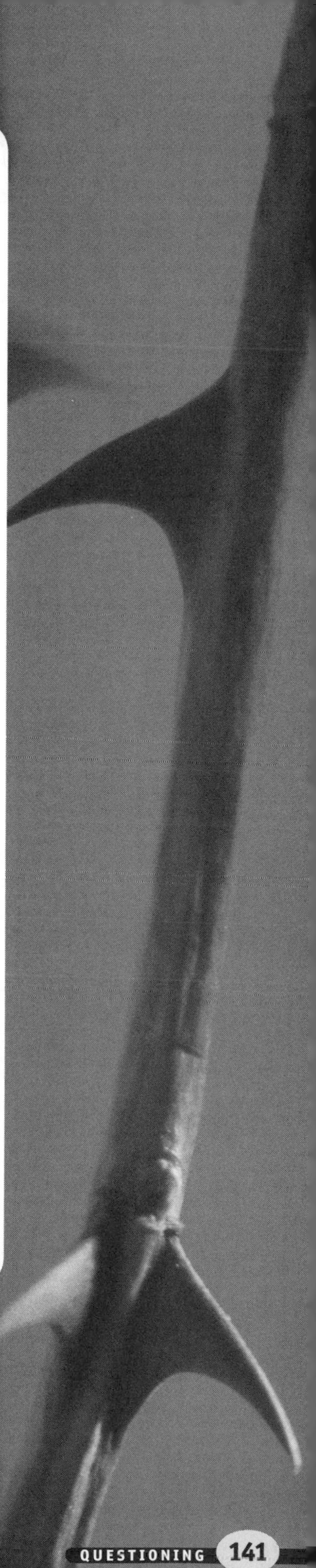

45 ADAPTING A TEXT

The best way to learn how visual texts work is to create your own. Art Spiegelman chose the graphic novel as the original form for *Maus*. But graphic novels may also be adapted from short stories or novels. In this lesson, you will create visual panels for a segment of another Holocaust story.

One of the best-known stories of the Holocaust is Anne Frank's diary. The diary tells of the years that Anne (shown left), her family, and others hid in Amsterdam. Anne's story ends when they are discovered and sent to a concentration camp. Her childhood friend, Hannah (who appears as Lies or Hanneli in the published diary), adds to what we know about Anne Frank. She shared her memories with Alison Gold, who wrote *Memories of Anne Frank: Reflections of a Childhood Friend*.

Hannah, who is also in a camp, has learned that Anne Frank is just on the other side of the fence. When the excerpt starts, she has been visiting her father in the hospital. As you read the excerpt, determine what is important and what you might leave out of your graphic text. In the **Response Notes,** jot down some ideas of what to use in a visual presentation of this excerpt.

Response Notes

from **Memories of Anne Frank** by Alison Gold

When Hannah got back to the barracks, there was great excitement. Packages were being distributed. This had never happened before. The packages were from the Red Cross. Hannah was given two packages for her family. One she immediately hid in order to bring it to her father in the hospital.

The packages were small boxes, the shape and size of a book. When she opened hers, she found dry, fried Swedish bread and dried fruit. Quietly she made a package of things for Anne.

Mrs. Abrahams saw Hannah on her way out of the barracks. She warned her that she mustn't go to the fence again. Once she had been lucky but she might not be so lucky again. Hannah explained that she had made contact with her best friend from her childhood. She told Mrs. Abrahams about Anne Frank, what terrible conditions were on the other side of the fence. Immediately Mrs. Abrahams handed Hannah a few scraps of food to put in the package.

The package consisted of a glove, some Swedish bread and dried fruit, and what she had saved from the evening meal. Hannah waited until it was dark and walked across the camp to the barbed-wire fence. Cautiously she whispered, "Anne? Are you there?"

Immediately the reply came, "Yes, Hanneli, I'm here."

Anne's voice was shaky, and she told Hannah that she had been waiting. Hannah told her she had scrounged up a few things and would throw them over to her.

Hannah felt very weak but summoned her strength and threw the package over the fence.

Immediately there was scuffling noise. Then the sound of someone running and Anne cried out in anguish.

"What happened?"

Anne was crying. "A woman ran over and grabbed it away from me. She won't give it back."

Hannah called, "Anne! I'll try again but I don't know if I'll be able to get away with it."

Anne was crushed.

Hannah begged her not to lose heart, "I'll try. In a few nights. Wait for me."

"I'll wait, Hanneli."

Hannah dashed across the snow, avoiding the searchlight. ❖

The next time Hannah sneaks to the fence, Anne does receive the package. After that, the people in her camp are moved, and Hannah never sees her again.

✳ In the space below, plan your visual text for this excerpt. Decide on the message you want to convey to readers. How will you draw the characters or emphasize what is important?

✳ Review your plan, and draw as much of the new visual text as you can below. If you do not want to draw, you can use computer graphics or magazine cutouts for the visuals.

A good way to understand how visual texts work is to create your own.

Making Connections

A well-written story keeps you involved. Suspense and mystery increase your curiosity and interest. You wonder what will happen next. A character who is in a difficult situation may gain your sympathy. Stories can be more than just entertainment or a great escape, though. The writing often has something to "say" to the reader. The idea or point a writer explores in a story is the **theme,** the underlying idea or meaning.

Writers almost always have more than one theme that they want to convey in any piece of writing. One way to think about theme is to imagine that you are having a conversation with the writer. Think to yourself, "What is the writer saying to me?" Chances are good that when you "listen" to the answer, you'll have found at least one of the themes.

46 CONNECTING DETAILS TO THEME

Themes in a piece of writing are the author's underlying statements about life or human nature. Most of the time, the writer does not directly state the **themes.** Instead, you have to read between the lines and figure out what the important ideas are. How can you find the themes? Here are some possibilities:

- Look to see if a theme is stated directly.

- Consider the details the writer emphasizes. If a certain character, for example, acts angry and as a result has no friends, what might the writer be trying to say?

- Read a chunk of the text and then stop and ask: "What is the writer saying to me?" Consider how the details and chunks add up to what is not stated.

When My Name Was Keoko is **historical fiction** that describes the Japanese occupation of Korea. The following excerpt is from the opening chapter which is narrated by a young girl named Sun-hee. Examine **details** as one way to figure out themes. Underline parts of the text that indicate the theme(s). In the **Response Notes,** make notes about what is emphasized.

from **When My Name Was Keoko** by Linda Sue Park

1. Sun-hee (1940)

"It's only a rumor," Abuji said as I cleared the table. "They'll never carry it out."

My father wasn't talking to me, of course. He was talking to Uncle and my brother, Tae-yul, as they sat around the low table after dinner, drinking tea.

I wasn't supposed to listen to men's business, but I couldn't help it. It wasn't really my fault. Ears don't close the way eyes do.

I worked slowly. First I scraped the scraps of food and dregs of soup into an empty serving dish. Then I stacked the brass bowls—quietly, so they wouldn't clang against one another. Finally, I moved around the table and began putting the bowls through the little low window between the sitting room and the kitchen. The kitchen was built three steps down from the central courtyard, and the sitting room three steps up. From the window I could reach a shelf in the kitchen. I put the bowls on the shelf one at a time, arranging them in a very straight line.

The longer I stayed in the room, the more I'd hear.

Uncle shook his head. "I don't know, Hyungnim," he said, disagreeing respectfully. "They're masters of organization—if they want this done, you

Response Notes

© GREAT SOURCE. COPYING IS PROHIBITED.

can be sure they will find a way to do it. And I fear what will happen if they do. Our people will not stand for it. I am afraid there will be terrible trouble—"

Abuji cleared his throat to cut off Uncle's words. He'd noticed me kneeling by the table with the last of the bowls in my hands; I was listening so hard that I'd stopped moving. Hastily, I shoved the bowl through the window and left the room, sliding the paper door closed behind me.

What rumor? What was going to happen? What kind of trouble?

When I asked Tae-yul later, he said it was none of my business. That was his answer a lot of the time. It always made me want to clench my fists and stamp my foot and hit something.

✳ Look at the details the author provides. Circle or underline places that might be clues to the theme or themes.

✳ Write a paragraph that describes possible themes and explain your reasons for what you chose.

_____

_____

_____

_____

Continue reading from the opening chapter.

They'll never carry it out. . . . They're masters of organization... I knew who "they" were. The Japanese. Whenever there was talk that I wasn't supposed to hear, it was almost always about the Japanese.

A long time ago, when Abuji was a little boy and Uncle just a baby, the Japanese took over Korea. That was 1910. Korea wasn't its own country anymore.

The Japanese made a lot of new laws. One of the laws was that no Korean could be the boss of anything. Even though Abuji was a great scholar, he was only the vice-principal of my school, not the principal. The person at the top had to be Japanese. The principal was the father of my friend Tomo.

All our lessons were in Japanese. We studied Japanese language, culture, and history. Schools weren't allowed to teach Korean history or language. Hardly any books or newspapers were published in Korean. People weren't even supposed to tell old Korean folktales. But Uncle did sometimes—funny stories about foolish donkeys or brave tigers, or exciting ones about heroes like Tan-gun, the founder of Korea. Tae-yul and I loved it when Uncle told us stories.

We still spoke Korean at home, but on the streets we always had to speak Japanese. You never knew who might be listening, and the military guards could punish anyone they heard speaking Korean. They usually didn't bother older people. But my friends and I had to be careful when we were in public.

Every once in a while another new law was announced, like the one when I was little that required us to attend temple on the Emperor's birthday. I decided that this must be the rumor—Abuji and Uncle had heard about a new law.

I was right. ✤

✂ **What do you think Park is saying about life in Korea during the Japanese occupation? Do a quick-write that answers this question. Explain what details in the story lead you to this understanding.**

_____

_____

_____

_____

_____

✂ **What details from the story point to the themes you've identified? For each of these details, jot down your ideas about how it supports a potential theme.**

Supporting Details	Theme
"I wasn't supposed to listen . . . "	The unequal position of men and women in this family or society

> Examine details that contribute to potential themes and ask yourself, "What is the writer saying to me?"

Often, stories that interest us have memorable events. But how do we as readers learn about themes through these events? Rarely does the writer come out and tell us all we need to know. Instead, writers let the events and actions, as well as the characters' reactions, give us clues about the themes. Think about why a writer includes a particular event in his or her story. It might be to illustrate an aspect of the message he or she is trying to convey.

In *When My Name Was Keoko,* Chapter 2 is narrated by Tae-yul, Sun-hee's brother. He tells how the Japanese have made another law affecting the Koreans. In your **Response Notes,** jot what you think this event reveals about the themes that surface in the novel.

from **When My Name Was Keoko** by Linda Sue Park

Response Notes

2. Tae-yul

Sun-hee is a real pain sometimes. Always asking questions, always wanting to know what's going on. I tell her it's none of her business, which is true. Abuji would tell her if he wanted her to know.

But I don't know what's happening either. Why hasn't he told me? It's not like I'm a little kid anymore—I'm old enough to know stuff.

One day I get home from school and Uncle comes in right after me. He's early, it's way before dinnertime. He's got a newspaper in one hand, and he walks right past me without even saying hello. "Hyungnim!" he calls.

Abuji is in the sitting room. Uncle goes in and closes the door behind him. I listen hard, but I can't hear anything—until Uncle raises his voice. "I won't do it!" he shouts. "They can't do this—they can't take away our names! I am Kim Young-chun, I will never be anyone else!"

Omoni and Sun-hee come out of the kitchen and look at me. I turn away a little, annoyed that I don't know what's going on. Just then Abuji opens the door and waves his hand toward us. So we all go into the room. Uncle is pacing around like crazy.

Abuji reads out loud from the newspaper: "'By order of the Emperor, all Koreans are to be graciously allowed to take Japanese names!'"

"'Graciously allowed…'" Uncle says. His voice is shaking, he's so mad. "How dare they twist the words! Why can't they at least be honest—we are being *forced* to take Japanese names!"

Abuji reads some more to himself, then says, "We must all go to the police station in the next week to register."

Uncle curses and pounds his fist against the wall.

My name, Tae-yul, means "great warmth." My grandfather—Abuji's father—chose it. It's one of our traditions for the grandfather to do the naming. He'd taken it seriously, Omoni once told me; he wanted a name that would bring me good fortune.

For Sun-hee, too—"girl of brightness."

A different name? I can't imagine it. I look at Sun-hee and I can tell she's thinking the same thing.

"Those who do not register will be arrested," Abuji says.

"Let them! Let them arrest me! They will have my body but not my soul—my name is my soul!" Uncle's face is red as a pepper.

Abuji holds up his hand. "Such talk is useless. It must be done. But let me think a while."

We leave him alone. I'm last out of the room, but I don't close the door. I watch him take a few books from the cupboard and turn the pages. Then he gets up again and fetches paper and pencil. Writes something on the paper, looks at it, writes some more. What's he doing?

At last he calls us all back into the room. Sun-hee and I sit on the floor, but Uncle stays standing, his arms crossed. Stubborn. Abuji waits a few moments, until Uncle seems calmer and uncrosses his arms.

"Tae-yul, Sun-hee, you know that the Kim clan is a large and important one," Abuji says. "Long ago, all Kims lived in the same part of Korea, in the mountains. Choosing the word for gold as their name shows what a strong clan they were. Gold was only for kings."

He picks up the sheet of paper from the table and points at it. "I have chosen our Japanese name. It will be Kaneyama. *'Yama'* means 'mountain' in Japanese, and *'ka-ne'* means 'gold.' So the name will honor our family history."

He turns to Uncle. "*They* will not know this. But we will."

Uncle doesn't look so mad now. "Kaneyama," he says quietly, and bows his head. "Hyungnim has chosen well."

"As to our first names," Aduji says, "Sun-hee, fetch your primer."

Sun-hee goes to the cupboard and brings back an old book. I know the book—it was mine first, then hers. The Japanese alphabet is on the first page. Abuji takes the book and opens it.

"We will close our eyes and point. Whatever letter we point to, we will choose a name that begins with this letter. These are not our real names, so we do not care what they are."

Uncle grins. "That's very good, Hyungnim. In fact, I do not care at all—you may choose my letter for me."

Abuji smiles, too. "No, we will each choose for ourselves."

First Abuji, then Uncle. My turn. I close my eyes. Point my finger any old way, and then look.

N. My new initial.

My new name: Kaneyama Nobuo. ❖

✳ What does this renaming event reveal about the themes in this novel? After you write your thoughts, share them with a partner.

_____

_____

_____

Another way of understanding themes is to put yourself in the position of the characters.

✳ Imagine that you are forced to change your name. You object and are told that you must write a letter explaining why you don't want to change your name. In your letter you need to answer the following questions: What does your name mean to you? What is the history of how you got your name? If you are still required to change your name, what new name would you take and why?

_____

_____

_____

_____

_____

_____

_____

_____

_____

_____

_____

_____

_____

Determine how events reveal themes in the story and explain how these events help you understand the themes conveyed.

IMAGES AND SYMBOLS SUGGEST THEMES

Look for images or symbols that suggest the themes of a story. A written **image** creates a picture in your mind that emphasizes something the writer wants you to notice. A **symbol** shows how one thing can represent something else. As you read another excerpt from *When My Name Was Keoko,* circle or underline images or symbols that you think suggest themes.

from **When My Name Was Keoko** by Linda Sue Park

Response Notes

7. Sun-hee

...Along the back of the vegetable patch was a row of small trees. Really, they were more like large shrubs. In the summer they blossomed—big pink—or white-petaled flowers with magenta throats. They were rose of Sharon trees, the national tree of Korea. Omoni had planted them years before, when she and Abuji had first moved to this house.

One evening in the fall Uncle brought home more news. The government had issued another official order. All families who had cherry trees were to dig up shoots and saplings from around their trees and bring them to police headquarters. The little cherry trees were to be planted all over town, and everyone was supposed to take good care of them.

The government order spoke of wishing to make our land more beautiful, with thousands of cherry trees. But it wasn't just a wish for beauty. The cherry tree was a national symbol of Japan.

And the final part of the order was that all rose of Sharon trees had to be uprooted and burned. The military police would be inspecting gardens to see that the order had been followed.

Omoni stayed inside the house; she couldn't bear to watch as Tae-yal chopped down the rose of Sharon trees one by one and dug out their roots. It was a difficult job; the trees were old and their roots reached deep into the ground. I helped him by dragging the fallen trees to a corner of the yard, where they'd be burned later.

Tae-yul had reached the last tree—a small one that Omoni had planted only a few years before. As he began to dig, Omoni came out of the house and said, "Tae-yul, wait. First go fetch a big pot, or a basin or something."

"What kind of pot?"

"I don't know—it needs to be big. Oh, wait—where you keep the tools, there's an old ceramic pot, with a crack in it. That will do."

I helped Tae-yul carry the pot out to her. It was quite large, as large around as my two arms could make a circle.

"Now," Omoni said, pointing to the last little tree. "Dig in a circle, and be careful not to cut any of the roots. I want you to bring the whole root ball out of the ground."

This took a long time. Tae-yul had used an ax to chop up the roots of the other trees and make it easier to dig them out. Now he could only use the shovel. Omoni returned to the house, but she came out from time to time to watch him work.

At last he put down the shovel and wiped his brow. "I think I can get it out now," he said. Although it had been the smallest tree, it was nearly as tall as me. Tae-yul pulled it carefully out of the hole and laid it down on the ground.

"Omoni!" I called.

She came out again and patted Tae-yul's shoulder. "You did a good job," she said. She walked around the little tree. "I think you will need to cut off about this much—" She pointed to a spot about a third of the way down from the top.

While Tae-yul chopped away with the ax, Omoni took up the shovel and began to fill the ceramic pot with dirt from where the tree had been dug up. Now I knew what she was doing. I got a trowel from the tool shelf and helped scoop dirt into the pot.

Omoni and Taw-yul lifted the little tree and settled it into the pot. Then we packed more dirt and mulch around it. Finally I fetched a basin of water and gave the tree a drink.

The three of us stepped back and looked at the tree and then at each other. We were tired and dirty, but we managed to smile. We'd hardly spoken throughout the entire task, yet we'd all known what to do. It felt good to have done this together. ❖

✳ What images stand out in your mind after reading this excerpt? Sketch at least two.

✳ What do the images you sketched tell you about potential themes in the story? When you finish, share your sketches and explanation with a partner.

_____

_____

_____

_____

_____

✳ Reflect on the two questions below. Record your ideas in the space provided.

What does Omoni's resistance to destroying the trees stand for, or symbolize, in the story? How does this reveal one of the themes?	What does the attempt of the Japanese to replace the rose of Sharon with cherry trees suggest about the themes of the story?

Look for images and symbols that contribute to the themes and decide what each contributes to your understanding of the story.

Stories are not the only types of writing that have themes. Poets convey **themes** in their poetry. And, unlike a story or novel in which the writer has a lot of space to develop themes, a poet has to get to the point much more quickly. As you read a poem, you can use the same strategies for finding themes that you used when reading stories. Look for details, events, symbols, and images that contribute to the themes just as you did in the previous lessons.

At about the same time that the Korean adolescents, Sun-hee and Tae-yul, experienced the Japanese control over their lives, another young person was feeling the effects of war. Vera lived in the Aleutian Islands off the coast of Alaska. For nine thousand years the Aleut people had lived on these islands. Suddenly, the entire population was forced into relocation centers by the U.S. government when the Japanese Navy invaded. Vera's story is told in a series of poems that are written in unrhymed verse. The poems are collected in a book called *Aleutian Sparrow*.

As you read the following poems, jot in the **Response Notes** column your thoughts about possible themes.

And So It Begins: The First Stop on Our Journey by Karen Hesse

In this temporary camp surrounded by trees on the
    grounds of Wrangell Institute
We have little else but the alphabet.
And so we gather together, five villages of Aleuts,
    and start stringing up the lanterns of our lives,
Story by story.

Response Notes

✳ What do you think Vera means by "stringing up the lanterns of our lives"? What is she saying in this poem about the theme of recognizing what is important in life?

_____

_____

_____

_____

Response Notes

Arrival at Ward Lake by Karen Hesse

Not until we are abandoned in the dark suffocation of the
forest,
Not until we count only two small bunkhouses and two
cabins for five villages of Aleuts,
Not until the morning, when we wake, on the floor, a
landscape of bedrolls and blankets,
Do we discover that we cannot, from any corner of the camp,
catch a glimpse of open water.

What images does this poem bring to mind? What do you think these images might suggest about the themes of this poem?

Blanket Houses by Karen Hesse

We have to choose between warmth
And privacy.
We hang blankets to divide the space inside the crowded
cabins.
I sleep beside my mother, not quite touching. And we shiver.

What does this poem suggest is important in life? What makes you think so?

✳ Begin to plan a poem of your own that reveals an important theme. Think of an event from your life that taught you something important. Elaborate about the event and the details of the event in the chart below. Can you think of symbols or images that would represent that theme? In the chart below, plan a poem about the event.

Brief description of the event	Important details that convey themes
Why the event is important and what themes it reveals	Symbols or images that suggest themes

✳ Write your poem in the space below.

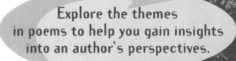

Explore the themes in poems to help you gain insights into an author's perspectives.

PERSPECTIVE AND THEME

A writer's themes provide insights into his or her perspectives. Themes often make a statement about life, the world, or human nature. Themes are more obvious when you are reading **personal narrative,** that is, when the author is talking about his or her own life.

The following excerpt is from a diary written by Zlata, a thirteen-year-old girl who began keeping her diary in September of 1991. In early entries of the diary, Zlata has a very typical preteen life. Then war breaks out in her city of Sarajevo. Life changes. In your **Response Notes,** jot down your thoughts about the possible themes revealed in Zlata's diary entries.

Response Notes

from Zlata's Diary: A Child's Life in Sarajevo
by Zlata Filipovic

Sunday, October 6, 1991
I'm watching the American Top 20 on MTV. I don't remember a thing, who's in what place.

I feel great because I've just eaten a "Four Season" PIZZA with ham, cheese, ketchup and mushrooms. It was yummy. Daddy bought it for me at Galija's (the pizzeria around the corner). Maybe that's why I didn't remember who took what place—I was too busy enjoying my pizza.

I've finished studying and tomorrow I can go to school BRAVELY, without being afraid of getting a bad grade. I deserve a good grade because I studied all weekend and I didn't even go out to play with my friends in the park. The weather is nice and we usually play "monkey in the middle," talk and go for walks. Basically, we have fun.

Monday, March 30, 1992
Hey, Diary! You know what I think? Since Anne Frank called her diary Kitty, maybe I could give you a name too. What about:

ASFALTINA	PIDZAMETA
SEFIKA	HIKMETA
SEVALA	MIMMY

Or something else???
    I'm thinking, thinking . . .
    I've decided! I'm going to call you
    MIMMY
    All right, then let's start.

Dear Mimmy,

It's almost half-term. We're all studying for our tests. Tomorrow we're supposed to go to a classical music concert at the Skendaerija Hall. Our teacher says we shouldn't go because there will be 10,000 people, pardon me, children, there, and somebody might take us as hostages or plant a bomb in the concert hall. Mommy says I shouldn't go. So I won't.

Hey! You know who won the Yugovision Song Contest? EXTRA NENA!!!???

I'm afraid to say this next thing. Melica says she heard at the hairdresser's that on Saturday, April 4, 1992, there's going to be BOOM—BOOM, BANG—BANG, CRASH Sarajevo. Translation: they're going to bomb Sarajevo.
Love, Zlata

Sunday, April 5, 1992
Dear Mimmy,

I'm trying to concentrate so I can do my homework (reading), but I simply can't. Something is going on in town. You can hear gunfire from the hills. Columns of people are spreading out from Dobrinja. They're trying to stop something, but they themselves don't know what. You can simply feel that something is coming, something very bad. On TV I see people in front of the B-H parliament building. The radio keeps playing the same song: "Sarajevo, My Love." That's all very nice, but my stomach is still in knots and I can't concentrate on my homework anymore.

Mimmy, I'm afraid of WAR!!!
Zlata

Monday, June 29, 1992
BOREDOM!!! SHOOTING!!! SHELLING!!! PEOPLE BEING KILLED!!! DESPAIR!!! HUNGER!!! MISERY!!! FEAR!!!

That's my life! The life of an innocent eleven-year-old schoolgirl!! A schoolgirl without a school, without the fun and excitement of school. A child without games, without friends, without the sun, without birds, without nature, without fruit, without chocolate or sweets, with just powdered milk. In short, a child without a childhood. A wartime child. I now realize that I am really living through a war, I am witnessing an ugly, disgusting war. I and thousands of other children in this town that is being destroyed, that is crying, weeping, seeking help, but getting none. God, will this ever stop, will I ever be a schoolgirl again, will I ever enjoy my childhood again? I once heard that childhood is the most wonderful time of your life. And it is. I loved it, and now an ugly war is taking it all away from me. Why? I feel sad. I feel like crying. I am crying.
Your Zlata

✳ What insight about Zlata's perspectives on life are revealed through her diary entries? Tell what sentences in the entries provide evidence of these perspectives. Explain.

_____

_____

_____

_____

✳ What themes are revealed through Zlata's perspectives on the war?

_____

_____

_____

_____

✳ Imagine that you are keeping a diary. You want to record what you have learned about young people whose lives have changed because of wars in their regions. Think about the young people you've just read about—Sun-hee, Tae-yul, Vera, and Zlata. In your diary entry, describe your reactions to what you have learned about their experiences during times of war. What themes of war have you discovered as a result of your reading in this unit?

In an author's personal story, explore the themes to help you gain insight into the writer's perspective.

Exploring Multiple Perspectives

When people want to persuade you to think a certain way, they want you to see the issue from a particular **perspective**—theirs! For **powerful persuasion,** writers or speakers use several techniques to convince their audience or move them to action. Historical figures such as Thomas Paine helped convince early American colonists that they should fight the British for their freedom. César Chavez convinced migrant farm workers to join a union, and they convinced grape growers to provide better wages and benefits to their workers. Rosa Parks spoke loudly about segregation through her quiet action of keeping her seat on a Birmingham, Alabama, bus. Powerful persuaders use language and action to convince others.

In this unit, you will learn about tools that persuaders use to structure their **arguments**—thesis statements and supporting evidence, tone, style, and emotional appeals. You will also have a chance to experiment with the power of persuasion.

The main idea of an argument may be expressed in a thesis statement. When you are able to identify the **thesis statement**, you understand what the author wants you to do or think. You also begin to understand what perspective the author has on the topic. The thesis may be implied rather than stated directly, but the main idea is always clear in an effective argument.

To be persuasive, the author also must provide **reasons** and **evidence.** As a reader or listener, you evaluate the reasons and evidence to see if they are convincing.

Read the letter from the Grand Council Fire of American Indians to the mayor of Chicago. Watch for the main idea and how it is supported. The thesis is directly stated twice. In the **Response Notes,** put a star by the thesis statements and mark any reasons that support the main idea.

"Memorial and Recommendations of the Grand Council Fire of American Indians"

Response Notes

December 1, 1927

To the mayor of Chicago:

You tell all white men "America First." We believe in that.

We are the only ones, truly, that are one hundred percent. We therefore ask you, while you are teaching schoolchildren about America First, teach them truth about the First Americans.

We do not know if school histories are pro-British, but we do know that they are unjust to the life of our people—the American Indian. They call all white victories battles and all Indian victories massacres. The battle with Custer has been taught to schoolchildren as a fearful massacre on our part. We ask that this, as well as other incidents, be told fairly. If the Custer battle was a massacre, what was Wounded Knee?

History books teach that Indians were murderers—is it murder to fight in self-defense? Indians killed white men because white men took their lands, ruined their hunting grounds, burned their forests, destroyed their buffalo. White men penned our people on reservations, then took away the reservations. White men who rise to protect their property are called patriots—Indians who do the same are called murderers.

White men call Indians treacherous—but no mention is made of broken treaties on the part of the white man. White men say that Indians were always fighting. It was only our lack of skill in white man's warfare that led to our defeat. An Indian mother prayed that her boy be a great medicine man rather than a great warrior. It is true that we had our own small battles, but in the main we were peace loving and home loving.

White men called Indians thieves—and yet we lived in frail skin lodges and needed no locks or iron bars. White men call Indians savages. What is civilization? Its marks are a noble religion and philosophy, original arts, stirring music, rich story and legend. We had these. Then we were not savages, but a civilized race.

We made blankets that were beautiful, that the white man with all his machinery has never been able to duplicate. We made baskets that were beautiful. We wove in beads and colored quills designs that were not just decorative motifs but were the outward expression of our very thoughts. We made pottery—pottery that was useful, and beautiful as well. Why not make schoolchildren acquainted with the beautiful handicrafts in which we were skilled? Put in every school Indian blankets, baskets, pottery.

We sang songs that carried in their melodies all the sounds of nature—the running of waters, the sighing of winds, and the calls of the animals. Teach these to your children that they may come to love nature as we love it.

We had our statesmen—and their oratory has never been equaled. Teach the children some of these speeches of our people, remarkable for their brilliant oratory.

We played games—games that brought good health and sound bodies. Why not put these in your schools? We told stories. Why not teach schoolchildren more of the wholesome proverbs and legends of our people? Tell them how we loved all that was beautiful. That we killed game only for food, not for fun. Indians think white men who kill for fun are murderers.

Tell your children of the friendly acts of Indians to the white people who first settled here. Tell them of our leaders and heroes and their deeds. Tell them of Indians such as Black Partridge, Shabbona, and others who many times saved the people of Chicago at great danger to themselves. Put in your history books the Indian's part in the World War. Tell how the Indian fought for a country of which he was not a citizen, for a flag to which he had no claim, and for a people that have treated him unjustly.

The Indian has long been hurt by these unfair books. We ask only that our story be told in fairness. We do not ask you to overlook what we did, but we do ask you to understand it. A true program of America First will give a generous place to the culture and history of the American Indian.

We ask this, Chief, to keep sacred the memory of our people. ❖

✳ Jot down your initial impressions about the letter. Is this letter interesting to you? Is it convincing? From your experience, do you think the same point could be made today?

_____

_____

_____

_____

✳ Good readers carefully evaluate the reasons and evidence that support a thesis. Are the reasons logical? Is there enough evidence to be convincing? Do the facts seem to be accurate? Facts, statistics, examples, observations, quotations, and experts' opinions all can provide **supporting evidence.** Use the following chart to show the reasons and evidence that support the thesis that school history books are "unjust to the life of . . . the American Indian." Label the kind of evidence used.

Reasons	Evidence
Indians are inaccurately portrayed as killers.	Indian victories are called "massacres"; white victories are called "battles."—observation
Indians are inaccurately portrayed as treacherous.	

This argument is/is not persuasive to me because _____

_____

_____

✳ Think of someone whom you feel is portrayed inaccurately. For example, you might think that the media show teenagers as lazy or unruly when that is not true. Briefly outline a letter that you could write to newspaper editors or to another audience to change people's minds. Be sure that your outline includes a thesis (your topic and what you want your audience to think or do about it), reasons, and evidence.

_____

_____

_____

_____

_____

_____

_____

_____

_____

_____

_____

_____

_____

_____

_____

_____

_____

_____

Understanding the structure of an argument helps you evaluate how persuasive it is.

LESSON 52 TONE

The author's tone can help you understand the author's perspective or opinion. **Tone** refers to the author's attitude toward the subject. It is created by the sentences and words that the author chooses to use. The tone can be described as solemn, angry, lighthearted, formal, casual, and so on. An author of a persuasive piece uses tone as a way of convincing you, the reader, to share his or her attitude.

As you read Abraham Lincoln's Gettysburg Address, think about his opinion and the tone of his speech. The Battle of Gettysburg, which took place in 1863, was one of the bloodiest of the Civil War. Five months after the battle ended, President Lincoln made this speech at a dedication ceremony to honor the thousands of soldiers who had died in that battle. In the audience were grief-stricken mothers, fathers, and children of the men who had died at Gettysburg.

Response Notes

Gettysburg Address by Abraham Lincoln

Four score and seven years ago our fathers brought forth on this continent, a new nation, conceived in Liberty, and dedicated to the proposition that all men are created equal.

Now we are engaged in a great civil war, testing whether that nation, or any nation so conceived and so dedicated, can long endure. We are met on a great battlefield of that war. We have come to dedicate a portion of that field as a final resting place for those who here gave their lives that that nation might live. It is altogether fitting and proper that we should do this.

But, in a larger sense, we cannot dedicate—we cannot consecrate—we cannot hallow—this ground. The brave men, living and dead, who struggled here have consecrated it, far above our poor power to add or detract. The world will little note, nor long remember what we say here, but it can never forget what they did here. It is for us the living, rather, to be dedicated here to the unfinished work which they who fought here have thus far so nobly advanced. It is rather for us to be here dedicated to the great task remaining before us—that from these honored dead we take increased devotion to that cause for which they gave the last full measure of devotion; that we here highly resolve that these dead shall not have died in vain; that this nation, under God, shall have a new birth of freedom; and that government of the people, by the people, for the people, shall not perish from the earth. ❖

✳ What two words would you use to describe Lincoln's tone?

_____   _____

✳ Reread the Gettysburg Address and circle the words that help establish the tone.

✳ Review the outline you developed at the end of Lesson 51. Decide what tone you want to use for the letter you will write and write the first paragraph, selecting words that will help you achieve that tone.

_____

_____

_____

_____

_____

_____

_____

_____

_____

_____

_____

_____

The tone of a piece of writing often reveals the author's opinion or feelings about the subject.

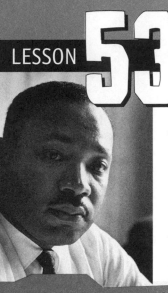

Persuaders know the power of choosing just the right words and arranging them in the most effective way. An author's style is his or her distinctive way of arranging words and constructing sentences. Even without a title or author, you can tell that the writer of the letter from the Grand Council Fire of American Indians is different from the writer of the Gettysburg Address.

In this lesson, you will read a speech that may already be familiar to you. As you read "I Have a Dream," circle words and phrases that seem to make up Martin Luther King, Jr.'s style.

Response Notes

"I Have a Dream" by Martin Luther King, Jr.

Five score years ago, a great American, in whose symbolic shadow we stand, signed the Emancipation Proclamation. This momentous decree came as a great beacon light of hope to millions of Negro slaves who had been seared in the flames of withering injustice. It came as a joyous daybreak to end the long night of captivity.

But one hundred years later, we must face the tragic fact that the Negro is still not free. One hundred years later, the life of the Negro is still sadly crippled by the manacles of segregation and the chains of discrimination. One hundred years later, the Negro lives on a lonely island of poverty in the midst of a vast ocean of material prosperity. One hundred years later, the Negro is still languishing in the corners of American society and finds himself an exile in his own land. So we have come here today to dramatize an appalling condition.

In a sense we have come to our nation's Capitol to cash a check. When the architects of our republic wrote the magnificent words of the Constitution and the Declaration of Independence, they were signing a promissory note to which every American was to fall heir. This note was a promise that all men would be guaranteed the unalienable rights of life, liberty, and the pursuit of happiness.

It is obvious today that America has defaulted on this promissory note insofar as her citizens of color are concerned. Instead of honoring this sacred obligation, America has given the Negro people a bad check; a check which has come back marked "insufficient funds." But we refuse to believe that the bank of justice is bankrupt. We refuse to believe that there are insufficient funds in the great vaults of opportunity of this nation. So we have come to cash this check—a check that will give us upon demand the riches of freedom and the security of justice. We have also come to this hallowed spot to remind America of the fierce urgency of now. This is no time to engage in the luxury of cooling off or to take the tranquilizing drug of gradualism. Now is the time to make real the promises of Democracy. Now is the time to rise from the dark and desolate valley of segregation to the sunlit path of racial justice. Now is the time to open the doors of opportunity to all of God's children. Now is the time to lift our nation from the quicksands of racial injustice to the solid rock of brotherhood.

It would be fatal for the nation to overlook the urgency of the moment and to underestimate the determination of the Negro. This sweltering summer of the Negro's legitimate discontent will not pass until there is an invigorating autumn of freedom and equality. 1963 is not an end, but a beginning. Those who hope that the Negro needed to blow off steam and will now be content will have a rude awakening if the nation returns to business as usual. There will be neither rest nor tranquility in America until the Negro is granted his citizenship rights. The whirlwinds of revolt will continue to shake the foundations of our nation until the bright day of justice emerges.

But there is something that I must say to my people who stand on the warm threshold which leads into the palace of justice. In the process of gaining our rightful place we must not be guilty of wrongful deeds. Let us not seek to satisfy our thirst for freedom by drinking from the cup of bitterness and hatred. We must forever conduct our struggle on the high plane of dignity and discipline. We must not allow our creative protest to degenerate into physical violence. Again and again we must rise to the majestic heights of meeting physical force with soul force. The marvelous new militancy which has engulfed the Negro community must not lead us to a distrust of all white people, for many of our white brothers, as evidenced by their presence here today, have come to realize that their destiny is tied up with our destiny and their freedom is inextricably bound to our freedom. We cannot walk alone.

And as we walk, we must make the pledge that we shall march ahead. We cannot turn back. There are those who are asking the devotees of civil rights, "When will you be satisfied?" We can never be satisfied as long as the Negro is the victim of the unspeakable horrors of police brutality. We can never be satisfied as long as our bodies, heavy with the fatigue of travel, cannot gain lodging in the motels of the highways and the hotels of the cities. We cannot be satisfied as long as the Negro's basic mobility is from a smaller ghetto to a larger one. We can never be satisfied as long as a Negro in Mississippi cannot vote and a Negro in New York believes he has nothing for which to vote. No, no, we are not satisfied, and we will not be satisfied until justice rolls down like waters and righteousness like a mighty stream.

I am not unmindful that some of you have come here out of great trials and tribulations. Some of you have come fresh from narrow jail cells. Some of you have come from areas where your quest for freedom left you battered by the storms of persecution and staggered by the winds of police brutality. You

have been the veterans of creative suffering. Continue to work with the faith that unearned suffering is redemptive.

Go back to Mississippi, go back to Alabama, go back to South Carolina, go back to Georgia, go back to Louisiana, go back to the slums and ghettos of our northern cities, knowing that somehow this situation can and will be changed. Let us not wallow in the valley of despair.

I say to you today, my friends, that in spite of the difficulties and frustrations of the moment I still have a dream. It is a dream deeply rooted in the American dream.

I have a dream that one day this nation will rise up and live out the true meaning of its creed: "We hold these truths to be self-evident; that all men are created equal."

I have a dream that one day on the red hills of Georgia the sons of former slaves and the sons of former slaveowners will be able to sit down together at the table of brotherhood.

I have a dream that the state of Mississippi, a desert state, sweltering with the heat of injustice and oppression, will be transformed into an oasis of freedom and justice.

I have a dream that my four little children will one day live in a nation where they will not be judged by the color of their skin but by the content of their character.

I have a dream today.

I have a dream that the state of Alabama, whose governor's lips are presently dripping with the words of interposition and nullification, will be transformed into a situation where little black boys and black girls will be able to join hands with little white boys and white girls and walk together as sisters and brothers.

I have a dream today.

I have a dream that one day every valley shall be exalted, every hill and mountain shall be made low, the rough places will be made plain, and the crooked places will be made straight, and the glory of the Lord shall be revealed, and all flesh shall see it together.

This is our hope. This is the faith with which I return to the South. With this faith we will be able to hew out of the mountain of despair a stone of hope. With this faith we will be able to transform the jangling discords of our nation into a beautiful symphony of brotherhood. With this faith we will be able to work together, to pray together, to struggle together, to go to jail together, to stand up for freedom together, knowing that we will be free one day.

This will be the day when all of God's children will be able to sing with new meaning, "My country, 'tis of thee, sweet land of liberty, of thee I sing. Land where my fathers died, land of the pilgrims' pride, from every mountainside, let freedom ring."

And if America is to be a great nation this must become true. So let freedom ring from the prodigious hilltops of New Hampshire. Let freedom ring from the mighty mountains of New York. Let freedom ring from the heightening Alleghenies of Pennsylvania!

Let freedom ring from the snowcapped Rockies of Colorado!

Let freedom ring from the curvaceous peaks of California! But not only that; let freedom ring from Stone Mountain of Georgia!

Let freedom ring from Lookout Mountain of Tennessee!

Let freedom ring from every hill and molehill of Mississippi. From every mountainside, let freedom ring.

When we let freedom ring, when we let it ring from every village and every hamlet, from every state and every city, we will be able to speed up that day when all of God's children, black men and white men, Jews and Gentiles, Protestants and Catholics, will be able to join hands and sing in the words of the old Negro spiritual, "Free at last! free at last! thank God Almighty, we are free at last!" ❖

※ What is your initial reaction to this speech? Which words or phrases stayed with you? Which moved you? How do you hear Dr. King's voice delivering this speech?

* Dr. King uses **allusion** and **repetition** to make his points and move his listeners to action. Allusions refer to other speeches, songs, and writings that the audience will recognize. Using allusions allows the author to connect his or her message to other ideas that the reader already knows and values. But the author also puts a new twist on the idea. For example, look at the beginning of the Gettysburg Address and the beginning of "I Have a Dream." Why do you think Dr. King started his speech as he did?

_____

_____

Repetition is used to emphasize or connect ideas and to direct attention to the variations. For example, many sentences begin with "I have a dream," but the dreams are all different. Because the sentences begin the same way, they reinforce the idea, but the listener begins to notice the differences, too.

* Reread "I Have a Dream" and highlight allusions in one color and repetitions in another.

* What is your opinion of the effectiveness of Dr. King's style in this speech?

_____

_____

_____

_____

_____

_____

_____

_____

_____

An author's style shapes and reinforces the persuasive message of a speech or a piece of writing.

Authors of persuasive arguments may choose to appeal to your feelings as well as to reason. Analyzing those appeals can help you evaluate the argument to determine how convincing it is. Authors sometimes use emotion-laden words to appeal to feelings. An author might want to anger you in order to convince you to act or to think a certain way. In another situation, an author might refer to basic values, such as kindness, justice, responsibility, freedom, or patriotism to persuade you. Both types of appeals can influence a reader's thinking. Critical readers must carefully evaluate the message to be sure they are not persuaded by just their feelings.

Words have two kinds of meanings—**denotation** and **connotation**. The denotation of a word is the dictionary meaning. The connotation is something suggested by a word. For example, the word *freedom* has emotional associations that go beyond the word's literal meaning. A word's connotations can depend on the perspective of the person using it. Look back at Lesson 51 to see how speakers use their point of view to select words with the connotation they think will persuade the listener. If you support the view of the Native Americans, what would you call a fight in which people died? If you do not support their view, what might you call the fight?

Imagine that you want to compliment one person and criticize another one about their body shape and their position on an issue. You can use a connotation ladder to select the right words. In the space below, select words from the word bank and place them on the ladder ranging from most complimentary at the bottom to least complimentary on the top.

Skinny　　　　　　　**Firm**

Scrawny　　　　　　**Decisive**

Slender　　　　　　 **Stubborn**

✳ On the chart below, check the kinds of appeals you find in each piece of writing in this unit. Compare your findings with a partner and label each letter or speech where you find examples of each kind of appeal.

Appeals to Reason	"Memorial and Recommendations…"	"Gettysburg Address"	"I Have a Dream"
Observations			
Examples			
Facts			
Appeals to Emotion			
Emotional language			
Mention of basic values			

✳ Which of the writings in this unit is most convincing to you? How do the appeals that the author uses help persuade you?

_____

_____

_____

_____

_____

_____

_____

_____

_____

_____

Readers can evaluate an argument by examining its appeals to reason and to emotion.

You have learned many of the persuader's tools:

- Structure an argument with a thesis, reasons, and evidence.
- Select an appropriate tone.
- Use a style that helps you make your point.
- Appeal both to emotion and to reason.

✳ Plan a persuasive speech or letter of your own. You can finish the letter that you began in Lesson 52 or select a new topic.

Possible Topics

Year-round schools
Aid to disaster victims
Required summer reading
Another issue of interest
 to you

✳ Jot down notes before writing your letter or speech. Decide on the points you want to make.

✳ My topic: _____

✳ My argument: _____

✳ Points I want to make:

- _____

- _____

- _____

- _____

✳ Choose one key point from your notes. Apply any one of the persuader's tools such as an appeal to basic values or use of an appropriate tone. Write one paragraph that you can use in your speech or letter.

_____
_____
_____
_____
_____
_____
_____
_____
_____
_____
_____
_____
_____
_____
_____
_____
_____

Persuaders carefully select the right tools to help them persuade the audience of their point of view or to take an action.

Focusing on Language and Craft

Poetry is undergoing a big change in cities around the United States these days. Coffee-shops, book stores, libraries—they all have scheduled poetry readings, poetry slams, music and poetry gatherings. Poetry is returning to its roots, where verses were sung or chanted. People are putting the **voice** back into poetry.

Of course, many people still read poetry to themselves and for personal pleasure, but more and more people like to hear it read aloud. They want to hear the poet's voice or the reader's voice. Voice makes poetry come alive.

In this unit, you will "hear" the voice of poetry. You will read it aloud, create poems for two voices, make one poem out of two, and finally write your own poem in your own voice.

Paul Fleischman, the son of the well-known writer Sid Fleischman, grew up surrounded by the sound of language. His father regularly read chapters of his work to the family, and the family gave him suggestions about what should happen next in the story. From this experience, Paul Fleischman says, "We grew up knowing that words felt good in the ears and on the tongue, that they were as much fun to play with as toys." Music was also an important part of the Fleischman household. Fleischman and his mother played the piano, his sisters played the flute, and his father played the guitar. As an adult, Fleischman learned to play the recorder, and he even toured with a recorder group.

Fleischman's love for both music and language has shaped his writing. His books *I Am Phoenix, Joyful Noise,* and *Big Talk* are poems for two or four voices to read aloud, like different voices in a choir or a variety of instruments in an orchestra. Even in his novels and non-fiction books, Fleischman pays careful attention to the rhythm of his sentences and the sounds of the words he puts together. He has received many awards for his books, including the Newbery Medal in 1989 for *Joyful Noise.*

As children, Paul Fleischman and his sisters often biked around the streets and alleys of their hometown, Monterey, California, collecting thrown-out items from other people's trash cans. Fleischman still does this in a way, gathering together forgotten bits of history and quirky facts he learns from old books as he crafts a new piece of writing.

The two poems by Paul Fleischman in this lesson are from *Joyful Noise,* which has poems about the noises of insects. If you have never really listened to the noises of insects, pay close attention to these poems and you will "hear" them in a new way. It will take practice to be able to read this poem effectively because you and your partner have to keep an eye on two columns at one time. When words appear on the same line, they should be spoken together. In some cases, the line that is read together is the same; other times it is different. Think of the poem as music for two instruments or a piano piece for two hands.

Grasshoppers by Paul Fleischman

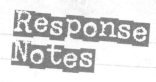

Sap's rising

       Ground's warming

Grasshoppers are
       Grasshoppers are
hatching out
       hatching out
Autumn-laid eggs

       splitting

Young stepping

       into spring

Grasshoppers
       Grasshoppers
hopping
       hopping
high
Grassjumpers
       Grassjumpers
jumping
       jumping
       far

Vaulting from
leaf to leaf
stem to stem
       leaf to leaf
plant to plant
       stem to stem
       Grass

leapers
       leapers
Grass-
bounders
       bounders
       Grass-

springers
       springers
Grass
soarers
       soarers
Leapfrogging
       Leapfrogging
longjumping
       longjumping
grasshoppers. ❖
       grasshoppers. ❖

❖ Practice reading the poem with a partner. Read the poem several times until you both are reading smoothly.

Here is another of Paul Fleischman's poems. Notice that, again, some lines are read by the first reader, some by the second, and some by both readers together. Practice reading with a partner.

Fireflies by Paul Fleischman

Response Notes

Light	Light
	is the ink we use
Night	Night
is our parchment	
	We're fireflies
fireflies	flickering
flitting	
	flashing
fireflies	
glimmering	fireflies
	gleaming
glowing	
Insect calligraphers	Insect calligraphers
practicing penmanship	
	copying sentences
Six-legged scribblers	Six-legged scribblers
of vanishing messages	
	fleeting graffiti
Fine artists in flight	Fine artists in flight
adding dabs of light	
	bright brush strokes
Signing the June nights	Signing the June nights
as if they were paintings	as if they were paintings
	We're
flickering	fireflies
fireflies	flickering
fireflies. ✤	fireflies. ✤

✳ After you and your partner have perfected your reading, get together with another pair and read to each other.

✳ Discuss the two poems by Paul Fleischman.

- Select words and phrases that you think are particularly effective.

- Talk about how the poems do or do not describe the grasshopper and the firefly.

  ✶ Are there people in your group who have never seen a firefly? Those who have should explain the firefly's appeal. Has anyone, for instance, ever caught them on a hot summer night and put them in a jar? What happens to them? Did you let them go?

  ✶ What are some other names for the grasshopper and the firefly?

- Talk about how the poems are like music for two voices or instruments.

✳ Working with a partner or group, compose your own poem for two voices.

- Select a subject.

- Write text for the left and right columns.

- Decide which lines you will say together.

- Copy your poem, then practice reading it before presenting the poem to the class.

Reading and writing poems for two voices helps you see how important sound is to poetry.

CREATING TWO VOICES FROM ONE

In Billy Collins's poem "On Turning Ten," we hear the voice of Billy, a ten-year-old. We also hear the voice of the grownup Billy, remembering how he thought when he was a child. First, just read or listen to the poem and try to hear echoes of a ten-year-old in the words.

Response Notes

"On Turning Ten" by Billy Collins

The whole idea of it makes me feel
like I'm coming down with something,
something worse than any stomach ache
or the headaches I get from reading in bad light—
a kind of measles of the spirit,
a mumps of the psyche,
a disfiguring chicken pox of the soul.

You tell me it is too early to be looking back,
but that is because you have forgotten
the perfect simplicity of being one
and the beautiful complexity introduced by two.
But I can lie on my bed and remember every digit.
At four I was an Arabian wizard.
I could make myself invisible
by drinking a glass of milk a certain way.
At seven I was a soldier, at nine a prince.

But now I am mostly at the window
watching the late afternoon light.
Back then it never fell so solemnly
against the side of my tree house,
and my bicycle never leaned against the garage
as it does today,
all the dark blue speed drained out of it.

This is the beginning of sadness, I say to myself,
as I walk through the universe in my sneakers.
It is time to say good-bye to my imaginary friends,
time to turn the first big number.

It seems only yesterday I used to believe
there was nothing under my skin but light.
If you cut me I would shine.
But now when I fall upon the sidewalks of life,
I skin my knees. I bleed. ❖

✳ Re-read the poem, using the **Response Notes** column to indicate where you hear the voice of the ten-year-old and where you hear a grownup remembering. Make notes, too, about any of your own memories of becoming a ten-year-old and your memories of being younger.

✳ Working with a partner, divide the poem into lines or phrases so that you can read it as a dialogue. Mark the poem so that two people can read it aloud.

✳ Read the poem to another pair of students, and then listen to them read their version. Talk about the different ways you chose to divide the poem.

✳ Write a paragraph that explains the way you and your partner chose to divide the poem.

Reading a poem in two voices helps you focus on the different voices within the poem.

58 MODELING A POEM

Modeling is a strategy that many writers use when they want to focus on the structure of a piece of writing. Writers may model prose or poetry. Modeling prose helps writers get inside the sentences. Modeling poetry can be useful when learning to write different kinds of poems. When you model a poem that has already been written, you are focusing on structure and meaning at the same time.

In this lesson, you will use the structure of Billy Collins's poem to give form to your own memories of being a different age.

✳ Reread your **Response Notes** about Billy Collins's poem "On Turning Ten" and look at the memories you recorded. Add more memories as they occur to you. Choose an age you want to start with; it might be "On Turning Thirteen" or "On Turning Eleven" or whatever age you choose. Fill in the chart, making up a poem of your own as you go. This is called **modeling.** You owe the structure of your poem to the original poet, but the ideas in your poem are yours.

"On Turning Ten" by Billy Collins	"On Turning _____" by _____
The whole idea of it makes me feel like I'm coming down with something, something worse than any stomach ache or the headaches I get from reading in bad light— a kind of measles of the spirit, a mumps of the psyche, a disfiguring chicken pox of the soul.	The whole idea of it makes me feel *(Write as many lines as you want here)*
You tell me it is too early to be looking back, but that is because you have forgotten the perfect simplicity of being one and the beautiful complexity introduced by two. But I can lie on my bed and remember every digit. At four I was an Arabian wizard. I could make myself invisible by drinking a glass of milk a certain way. At seven I was a soldier, at nine a prince.	You tell me _____, but that is because you have forgotten _____ and _____. But I can lie on my bed and remember every digit. At four I was _____. I could _____. At _____ I was _____, At _____ I was _____.

"On Turning Ten" by Billy Collins	"On Turning _____" by _____
But now I am mostly at the window watching the late afternoon light. Back then it never fell so solemnly against the side of my tree house, and my bicycle never leaned against the garage as it does today, all the dark blue speed drained out of it.	But now I _____ _____ . Back then _____ _____ , and my _____ never _____ _____ as it does today, _____ .
This is the beginning of sadness, I say to myself, as I walk through the universe in my sneakers. It is time to say good-bye to my imaginary friends, time to turn the first big number.	This is the beginning of _____ , I say, as I _____ . It is time to say good-bye _____ , time to _____ .
It seems only yesterday I used to believe there was nothing under my skin but light. If you cut me I would shine. But now when I fall upon the sidewalks of life, I skin my knees. I bleed. *by Billy Collins*	It seems only yesterday I used to _____ _____ _____ . But now when _____ , I _____ . *by _____ , with thanks to Billy Collins*

✳ Share your poem with your group and, perhaps, with the whole class.

Modeling is a strategy that makes you attend to the structure as well as the ideas of the original piece of writing.

You may have read all or part of one of Maya Angelou's best-known books, *I Know Why the Caged Bird Sings*. You may also have found her simple lyrical poems in greeting cards. Maya Angelou is a great inspiration to many people because she was able to survive a tough childhood to become a famous writer, actress, professor, historian, songwriter, playwright, dancer, and civil-rights activist.

Here are a few quotations from Maya Angelou's writing and talks:

- I speak to the black experience, but I am always talking about the human condition—about what we can endure, dream, fail at, and still survive.

- There is nothing so pitiful as a young cynic because he has gone from knowing nothing to believing nothing.

- If you don't like something, change it. If you can't change it, change your attitude. Don't complain.

- We need language to tell us who we are, how we feel, what we're capable of — to explain the pains and glory of our existence.

- If you have only one smile in you, give it to the people you love. Don't be surly at home, then go out in the street and start grinning "good morning" at total strangers.

In this lesson, you will read two of Maya Angelou's poems, then create a new poem from them by selecting words and phrases from each to make a poetic dialogue. You will then read your "hybrid" poem to the class.

Response Notes

Life Doesn't Frighten Me

Shadows on the wall
Noises down the hail
Life doesn't frighten me at all
Bad dogs barking loud
Big ghosts in a cloud
Life doesn't frighten me at all.

Mean old Mother Goose
Lions on the loose
They don't frighten me at all
Dragons breathing flame

Alone   by Maya Angelou

Lying, thinking
Last night
How to find my soul a home
Where water is not thirsty
And bread loaf is not stone
I came up with one thing
And I don't believe I'm wrong
That nobody,
But nobody
Can make it out here alone.

On my counterpane
That doesn't frighten me at all.

I go boo
Make them shoo
I make fun
Way they run
I won't cry
So they fly
I just smile
They go wild
Life doesn't frighten me at all.

Tough guys in a fight
All alone at night
Life doesn't frighten me at all.
Panthers in the park
Strangers in the dark
No, they don't frighten me at all.

That new classroom where
Boys pull all my hair
(Kissy little girls
With their hair in curls)
They don't frighten me at all.

Don't show me frogs and snakes
And listen for my scream,
If I'm afraid at all
It's only in my dreams.

I've got a magic charm
That I keep up my sleeve,
I can walk the ocean floor
And never have to breathe.

Life doesn't frighten me at all
Not at all
Not at all
Life doesn't frighten me at all. ❖

Alone, all alone
Nobody, but nobody
Can make it out here alone.
There are some millionaires
With money they can't use
Their wives run round like banshees
Their children sing the blues
They've got expensive doctors
To cure their hearts of stone.
But nobody
No, nobody
Can make it out here alone.
Alone, all alone
Nobody, but nobody
Can make it out here alone.
Now if you listen closely
I'll tell you what I know
Storm clouds are gathering
The wind is gonna blow
The race of man is suffering
And I can hear the moan,
'Cause nobody,
But nobody
Can make it out here alone.
Alone, all alone
Nobody, but nobody
Can make it out here alone. ◻

✳ With a partner, take turns reading both of Maya Angelou's poems aloud. Each of you should take major responsibility for one poem, but talk together as you work.

■ Talk about what each poem is saying.
  ✳ Who is the speaker?
  ✳ What is she or he saying?
  ✳ How are the two poems related?

■ Underline or highlight words, phrases, and lines that stand out for you.

■ From these two poems, create a new, "hybrid" poem that conveys the sense of each of the poems, but results in a completely new poem.

■ The chart that follows is a sample worksheet on which you can develop your new poem. Copy a blank version onto a piece of paper.
  ✳ Write words, phrases, or complete lines from the two poems in the appropriate column so that when you read them in two voices, they make a new kind of sense.
  ✳ You may use repetition, or you may vary the order in which the words appear, but use only the words of the two poems in your final poem.
  ✳ Write in only one column at a time so you will know when it is your turn to read the lines. See the lines selected for the chart below.
  ✳ Indicate whether the words are to be spoken by one person or by both. If they are to be spoken by both, write them in the center column.

Words and phrases from "Life Doesn't Frighten Me" (Speaker A)	Words and phrases to be read together, by both speakers (these can be from either poem)	Words and phrases from "Alone" (Speaker B)
Shadows on the wall		
		Lying, thinking
		How to find my soul
	Life doesn't frighten me at all.	

* Read the new poem with your partner as a dialogue, each reading the words from one of the poems, both reading the lines in the center column.

* Write a paragraph that tells how your understanding of the two Angelou poems was affected by the process of writing a new poem from them. Did your understanding of them change? If so, how?

_____

_____

_____

_____

_____

Creating a "hybrid" poem from two poems helps focus attention on the language and meaning of the original poems.

Getting Home Alive is a book of poems by Aurora Levins Morales and her mother Rosario Morales. In the *Introduction*, Aurora writes, "My mother taught me to read. At some point, interwoven with our book reviews, we began to read each other our writing as well." That early practice led to their collaboration on this book and, later, on the final poem in the book. Aurora and Rosario wrote alternating lines of "Ending Poem."

Divide into groups of 6-10 students each. In your group, have two people read alternating lines for the first stanza. Then have two others read the next stanza. Continue in that pattern through the rest of the poem.

Before you begin, practice saying these words:

mestiza (meh STEE zuh)	*negra* (NEG ruh)
diaspora (die AS por uh)	*ne* (neh)
jíbara (HEE buh ruh)	*caribeña* (car eh BEN ya)
shtetl (SHTET ul)	*Boricua* (bore ee KU uh)
mija (MEE huh)	*Taína* (TYE nuh)

Ending Poem by Rosario Morales and Aurora Levins Morales

Response Notes

I am what I am.
          A child of the Americas.
A light-skinned mestiza of the Caribbean.
          A child of many diaspora, born into this continent at a
          crossroads.
I am Puerto Rican. I am U.S. American.
          I am New York Manhattan and the Bronx.
A mountain-born, country-bred, homegrown jíbara child,
          up from the shtetl, a California Puerto Rican Jew
A product of the New York ghettos I have never known.
          I am an immigrant
and the daughter and granddaughter of many immigrants.
          We didn't know our forbears' names with a certainty.
They aren't written anywhere.
          First names only or mija, negra, ne, honey,
          sugar, dear
I come from the dirt where the cane was grown.
          My people didn't go to dinner parties.
          They weren't invited.
I am caribeña, island grown.

Spanish is in my flesh, ripples from my tongue,
lodges in my hips,
the language of garlic and mangoes.
Boricua. As Boricuas come from the isle of Manhattan.
I am of latinoamerica, rooted in the history of my continent.
I speak from that body.
Just brown and pink and full of drums inside.
I am not African.
Africa waters the roots of my tree, but I cannot return.
I am not Taína.
I am a late leaf of that ancient tree,
and my roots reach into the soil of two Americas.
Taína is in me, but there is no way back.
I am not European, though I have dreamt of those cities.
Each plate is different.
wood, clay, papier mâché, metals basketry, a leaf, a coconut shell.
Europe lives in me but I have no home there.
The table has a cloth woven by one, dyed by another,
embroidered by another still.
I am a child of many mothers.
They have kept it all going.
All the civilizations erected on their backs.
All the dinner parties given with their labor.
We are new.
They gave us life, kept us going,
brought us to where we are.
Born at a crossroads.
Come, lay that dishcloth down. Eat, dear, eat.
History made us.
We will not eat ourselves up inside anymore.
And we are whole. ❖

✳ This poem expresses many facets of the two women. It tells who
they are. Using your **Response Notes,** comment on the words
and phrases that define the mother and daughter. Look for and
label words that have to do with these aspects of life:

- Geography
- History
- Food
- Names
- Customs
- Language

❋ You know something about Rosario and Aurora Morales. What about you? Who are you? Use the following poem format and write a poem describing you. Notice that all the lines involve a particular verb. Verbs are words that show action. In this model, you will use both concrete images, as in "I hear…" or "I touch…" and abstractions, as in "I wonder…" or "I dream…" Notice, too, the importance of nouns, especially place words that are very much a part of "Ending Poem."

❋ Title your poem with a word or phrase that describes some aspect of who you are.

"I Am" Poem Format

I am *(2 special characteristics you have)*
I have lived *(name or list places you have lived)*
I am part of *(name family or group that you feel a part of)*
I treasure *(something you care a lot about)*
I wonder *(something you are curious about)*
I hear *(an imaginary sound)*
I want *(an actual desire)*
I pretend *(something you pretend to do)*
I feel *(a feeling about something imaginary)*
I am *(the first line of the poem repeated)*
I eat *(a few foods that are important to you)*
I touch *(an imaginary touch)*
I worry *(something that really bothers you)*
I cry *(something that makes you sad)*
I understand *(something you know is true)*
I say *(something you believe in)*
I dream *(something you dream about)*
I try *(something you really make an effort to do)*
I hope *(something you hope for)*
I am *(the first line of the poem repeated)*

You may want to make a clean copy of your poem and illustrate it with drawings or a border.

❋ Share your poems with each other in small groups or with the whole class.

> The power of poetry lies in word choice: in nouns that designate place and in verbs that show feeling and movement.

Studying an Author

Look around your classroom. Do you think anyone in your class will become a published author? You never know. When **Walter Dean Myers** was in school, maybe in a class like yours, no one—especially Walter Dean Myers—thought that he would be an author. Now he has published more than thirty novels for young adults, several works of nonfiction for young adults and children, and many picture books for children. The numerous awards for his writing include two Newbery Honor medals, Coretta Scott King Awards, a Michael L. Printz Award, and the Margaret A. Edwards Award for lifetime writing achievement. How could someone who was often in trouble in elementary school and who dropped out of high school become such a famous author? He liked to read and write and, once he knew what he wanted to do, he worked hard at it.

In this unit, you will read some of Walter Dean Myers's writing. By studying the author in depth, you will learn where his stories come from. Throughout the unit, you will have a chance to sharpen your own skills as an author. Who knows where that may lead?

Not all authors use their own lives as sources of material for their stories, but some do. Walter Dean Myers is one of them. When you know something about his background, you will have a better understanding of the stories he writes and the values his characters demonstrate. Walter Myers was born in Martinsburg, West Virginia, in August 1937. His mother died when he was two, and his father sent him to Harlem (a section of New York City) to live with foster parents, the Deans. To show his respect for them, he took their last name as his middle name when he became an adult.

Myers enjoyed his life in Harlem, but he also got into a lot of trouble. In fact, his memoir is titled *Bad Boy* because he was in trouble so much. In fifth grade he went to a new school where he made a poor impression on the teacher on the first day. His relationship with Mrs. Conway did not improve for some time. As you read the excerpt that follows, make check marks or notes in the **Response Notes** for anything Myers says that makes a connection to or reminds you of something in your life.

from **Bad Boy: A Memoir** by Walter Dean Myers

Response Notes

Being good in class was not easy for me. I had a need to fill up all the spaces in my life, with activity, with talking, sometimes with purely imagined scenarios that would dance through my mind, occupying me while some other student was at the blackboard. I did want to get good marks in school, but they were never of major importance to me, except in the sense of "winning" the best grade in a subject. My filling up the spaces, however, kept me in trouble. I would blurt out answers to Mrs. Conway's questions even when I was told to keep quiet, or I might roll a marble across my desk if she was on the other side of the room.

The other thing that got me in trouble was my speech. I couldn't hear that I was speaking badly, and I wasn't sure that the other kids did, but I knew they often laughed when it was my turn to speak. After a while I would tense up anytime Mrs. Conway called on me. I threw my books across that classroom enough times for Mrs. Conway to stop my reading aloud once and for all.

But when the class was given the assignment to write a poem, she did read mine. She said that she liked it very much.

"I don't think he wrote that poem," Sidney Aronofsky volunteered.

I gave Sidney Aronofsky the biggest punch he ever had in the back of his big head and was sent to the closet. After the incident with Sidney,

Mrs. Conway said that I would not be allowed to participate in any class activity until I brought my mother to school. I knew that meant a beating. I thought about telling Mama that the teacher wanted to see her, but I didn't get up the nerve. I didn't get it up the next day, either. In the meantime I had to sit in the back of the room, and no kid was allowed to sit near me. I brought some comic books to school and read them under my desk.

Mrs. Conway was an enormously hippy woman. She moved slowly and always had a scowl on her face. She reminded me of a great white turtle with just a dash of rouge and a touch of eye shadow. It was not a pretty sight. But somehow she made it all the way from the front of the room to the back, where I sat reading a comic, without my hearing her. She snatched the comic from me and tore it up. She dropped all the pieces on my desk, then made me pick them up and take them to the garbage can while the class laughed.

Then she went to her closet, snatched out a book, and put it in front of me.

"You are," she sputtered, "a bad boy. A very bad boy. You cannot join the rest of the class until your mother comes in." She was furious, and I was embarrassed.

"And if you're going to sit back here and read, you might as well read something worthwhile," she snapped.

I didn't touch the book in front of me until she had made her way back to the front of the class and was going on about something in long division. The title of the book was *East o' the Sun and West o' the Moon*. It was a collection of Norwegian fairy tales, and I read the first one. At the end of the day, I asked Mrs. Conway if I could take the book home.

She looked at me a long time and then said no, I couldn't. But I could read it every day in class if I behaved myself. I promised I would. For the rest of the week I read that book. It was the best book I had ever read. . . .

I realized I liked books, and I liked reading. Reading a book was not so much like entering a different world—it was like discovering a different language. It was a language clearer than the one I spoke, and clearer than the one I heard around me. . . . The "me" who read the books, who followed the adventures, seemed more the real me than the "me" who played ball in the streets. ❖

✳ **Do you agree that Walter was a "bad boy"? Why or why not?**

_____

_____

_____

_____

_____

✳ Look at the connections you marked in the **Response Notes.**
Use the connections to begin a story about yourself at school at
any time in your past. Or create the beginning of a story about a
new, fictional character who might have had an experience
similar to Myers's.

_____

_____

_____

_____

_____

_____

_____

_____

_____

_____

_____

_____

_____

_____

_____

_____

_____

Some authors get
material for their stories from
experiences in their lives.

Freedom is necessary for humans to have dignity, Walter Dean Myers seems to say in many of his books. It is a **theme** that Myers often uses. The African American characters in his books struggle for both dignity and freedom. They seek freedom from drugs, gangs, prison, and the abuses of white society's laws and prejudices. In *Harlem's Hellfighters,* Myers tells of African American troops who volunteered and fought bravely in World War I, even though white officers did not treat the black soldiers as equals. The black troops therefore served with the French instead of with Americans.

In *The Glory Field,* Myers tells the story of one family descended from an African slave who bought a piece of land and held onto it through several generations. Looking back on the time of slavery, a father says to his son, "Those shackles didn't rob us of being black, son, they robbed us of being human." As you read about Lizzy, a thirteen-year-old runaway slave girl and her friend Lem, mark examples of the search for freedom and dignity.

from The Glory Field by Walter Dean Myers

Response Notes

Lem and Lizzy stayed low as they moved toward the campfires. There were shadows among the fires, and once in a while they could make out a person. They couldn't see what they looked like.

"Hold it!"

Lizzy jumped and grabbed her arms. Lem started to run, and two men with rifles jumped in front of him. One swung his rifle, and Lizzy watched as Lem reeled backwards and fell heavily in the dark field.

"Contraband!" A voice near Lizzy spoke up.

Two other men went over and looked at Lem and then moved away.

"Get on into the camp if you want," the voice nearest Lizzy said.

Lizzy turned and saw the soldier. She couldn't believe her eyes. He was tall and broad-faced, and the rifle he carried looked almost taller than he was. But that wasn't what amazed Lizzy.

"You're black!" she said.

"Glad you noticed it," the soldier grinned. "I had just about forgot it."

Lizzy helped Lem up. Together they started toward the campfires.

"Are they Yankees?" Lem asked.

"I guess they are," Lizzy whispered. "They carrying guns, too!"

As they neared the fires they heard singing. It was black singing, all right, a low praise hymn being crooned sweet and strong in the night.

The Yankee camp was busy. The camp was filled with soldiers, half of them white, the others black.

Snatches of conversation drifted toward them. The voices weren't like the ones they had heard before, and Lizzy was having trouble understanding them. They seemed relaxed, busy with the work of soldiering. There were a lot of other blacks, too. Some of them were just sitting around; others were cleaning boots or saddles.

"You young folks looking for something to eat you can get it around by that wagon." An old man, his white beard contrasting sharply with his black skin, pointed toward a wagon.

"You got black soldiers here!" Lizzy said.

"There's four and forty thousand of them, seven hundred and threescore, all crying out to the Lord for strength," the old man said. "How can they fail?"

✳ **What two words would you use to describe Lizzy at this point?**

_____

_____

Lizzy and Lem are fed beans and bread in the camp and fall asleep. Lizzy dreams of her recent past—the hounds chasing the runaway slaves—and another dream that involves the 17-year-old white daughter of Lizzy's "owner."

But it was the other dream that filled her, that moved her body in her sleep. It was a dream of being free, of walking across a wide meadow, not even following a road, just going any which way she wanted to go, not caring when she got there. She had the dream over and over again, each time wearing a different one of Miss Julia's dresses. It was a beautiful dream.

✳ **What does this dream add to your picture of Lizzy? Add two more words to describe her.**

_____

_____

Now read what happens next, continuing to make notes about freedom and dignity. The soldiers—black and white—move out of camp. Lem has joined them.

"What should I do?" Lizzy looked around as the soldiers and wagons started moving out. "What am I going to do?"

"Girl, you can go on with some folks who gonna try to make it North," a woman said. "Or you can stay with the soldiers and help them do what they want. They always need somebody to cook and mend."

Lizzy looked to where the black soldiers had gone down a road, seeing them turn and disappear around a bend. She couldn't see around the bend, or know what she was going to find when she got around it, but she knew she had to find out.

She ran as fast as she could, her feet slapping against the hard road. When she got around the bend, the men were still in sight, tall and proud.

She followed them, never looking back. ❖

✳ How does Walter Dean Myers use the character of Lizzy to portray his theme of freedom and dignity?

_____

_____

_____

_____

_____

_____

_____

_____

_____

_____

_____

_____

_____

_____

_____

An author's theme can come to life through the characters in the story.

LESSON 63 PLOTTING CONSEQUENCES

Another theme that is important to Walter Dean Myers is dealing with the consequences of one's actions. He develops this theme by building a **plot** from a set of character traits. Lizzy's freedom dream helped her decide what to do. In *Scorpions,* seventh-grader Jamal accepts a gun from an older teen and everything changes. In *The Beast,* Gabi chooses drugs to help her deal with the problems in her life. Not surprisingly, more problems arise. The barber, Duke, in *Handbook for Boys,* could be speaking for Myers when he points out that life doesn't work, people have to. The people who succeed, according to him, are those who know what they want and are willing to work for it.

Sixteen-year-old Steve Harmon made a bad decision. Now he's on trial for murder. Is he guilty? Is he the monster the prosecutor makes him out to be, or was he just in the wrong place at the wrong time? As you read the opening journal entry in *Monster,* use the **Response Notes** space to make notes about Steve's character.

from **Monster** by Walter Dean Myers

Response Notes

The best time to cry is at night, when the lights are out and someone is being beaten up and screaming for help. That way even if you sniffle a little they won't hear you. If anyone knows that you are crying, they'll start talking about it and soon it'll be your turn to get beat up when the lights go out.

There is a mirror over the steel sink in my cell. It's six inches high, and scratched with the names of some guys who were here before me. When I look into the small rectangle, I see a face looking back at me but I don't recognize it. It doesn't look like me. I couldn't have changed that much in a few months. I wonder if I will look like myself when the trial is over.

. . .

They say you get used to being in jail, but I don't see how. Every morning I wake up and I am surprised to be here. If your life outside was real, then everything in here is just the opposite. We sleep with strangers, wake up with strangers, and go to the bathroom in front of strangers. They're strangers but they still find reasons to hurt each other.

Sometimes I feel like I have walked into the middle of a movie. It is a strange movie with no plot and no beginning. The movie is in black and white, and grainy. Sometimes the camera moves in so close that you can't tell what is going on and you just listen to the sounds and guess. I have seen movies of prisons but never one like this. This is not a movie about bars and locked

doors. It is about being alone when you are not really alone and about being scared all the time.

I think to get used to this I will have to give up what I think is real and take up something else. I wish I could make sense of it.

Maybe I could make my own movie. I could write it out and play it in my head. I could block out the scenes like we did in school. The film will be the story of my life. No, not my life, but of this experience. I'll write it down in the notebook they let me keep. I'll call it what the lady who is the prosecutor called me. Monster. ✷

✷ In this journal entry, Steve does not describe himself directly. You have to infer character traits from the thoughts he shares. Discuss with a partner the traits you wrote in the **Response Notes.** Add to your notes any traits you did not think of the first time you read.

Walter Dean Myers often works with groups of student writers. He helps them plot a story by "starting with a simple personality trait of a character and seeing how that character reacts to some crisis."

For example, if the character lacks self-confidence but wants to appear tough, he might be more likely to carry a gun to school. The crisis in the story could begin when he showed that gun to someone. Depending on who saw it, he or she might take any one of several actions, such as reporting him to authorities. The action would then lead to further consequences, and you would have a story.

✳ Try your hand at plotting a story that grows from a character trait. You can use Lizzy in Lesson 62, Steve, or a character you create. Tell the name of your character. In the chart below, list the character trait, briefly describe the crisis, and tell the character's reactions.

Name of Character _____

Character Trait	Crisis	Character's Reactions

The plot of a story can develop from the ways in which the character reacts to a crisis.

Walter Dean Myers is probably best known for his fiction about teenagers facing the obstacles of inner-city life. But he also writes **nonfiction,** presenting real men and women who, like his fictional characters, show the positive decisions that people can make in troubled circumstances.

In the following excerpt from *Now Is Your Time!* Walter Dean Myers describes a court case, *Brown vs. Board of Education of Topeka*. This case challenged the ruling that "separate but equal" schools for black and white students were constitutional. Thurgood Marshall was the attorney who spearheaded the case against segregation. (Marshall later served on the Supreme Court.) As you read, circle or highlight the names of the people whom Myers would call heroes.

from **Now Is Your Time!** by Walter Dean Myers

It was Thurgood Marshall and a battery of N.A.A.C.P. attorneys who began to challenge segregation throughout the country. These men and women were warriors in the cause of freedom for African Americans, taking their battles into courtrooms across the country. They understood the process of American justice and the power of the Constitution.

In *Brown vs. Board of Education of Topeka*, Marshall argued that segregation was a violation of the Fourteenth Amendment—that even if the facilities and all other "tangibles" were equal, which was the heart of the case in *Plessy vs. Ferguson,* a violation still existed. There were intangible factors, he argued, that made the education unequal.

Everyone involved understood the significance of the case: that it was much more than whether black children could go to school with white children. If segregation in the schools was declared unconstitutional, then all segregation in public places could be declared unconstitutional.

Southerners who argued against ending school segregation were caught up, as then-Congressman Brooks Hays of Arkansas put it, in "a lifetime of adventures in that gap between law and custom." The law was one thing, but most Southern whites felt just as strongly about their customs as they did the law.

Dr. Kenneth B. Clark, an African-American psychologist, testified for the N.A.A.C.P. He presented clear evidence that the effect of segregation was harmful to African-American children. Describing studies conducted by black and white psychologists over a twenty-year period, he showed that black children felt inferior to white children. In a particularly dramatic study that he had supervised, four dolls, two white and two black, were presented to

Response Notes

African-American children. From the responses of the children to the dolls, identical in every way except color, it was clear that the children were rejecting the black dolls. African-American children did not just feel separated from white children, they felt that the separation was based on their inferiority.

Dr. Clark understood fully the principles and ideas of those people who had held Africans in bondage and had tried to make slaves of captives. By isolating people of African descent, by barring them from certain actions or places, they could make them feel inferior. The social scientists who testified at *Brown vs. Board of Education* showed that children who felt inferior also performed poorly.

The Justice Department argued that racial segregation was objectionable to the Eisenhower Administration and hurt our relationships with other nations.

On May 17, 1954, after deliberating for nearly a year and a half, the Supreme Court made its ruling. The Court stated that it could not use the intentions of 1868, when the Fourteenth Amendment was passed, as a guide to its ruling, or even those of 1896, when the decision in *Plessy vs. Ferguson* was handed down. Chief Justice Earl Warren wrote:

We must consider public education in the light of its full development and its present place in American life throughout the nation. We must look instead to the effect of segregation itself on public education.

The Court went on to say that "modern authority" supported the idea that segregation deprived African Americans of equal opportunity. "Modern authority" referred to Dr. Kenneth B. Clark and the weight of evidence that he and the other social scientists had presented.

The high court's decision in *Brown vs. Board of Education* signaled an important change in the struggle for civil rights. It signaled clearly that the legal prohibitions that oppressed African Americans would have to fall. Equally important was the idea that the nature of the fight for equality would change. Ibrahima, Cinqué, Nat Turner, and George Latimer had struggled for freedom by fighting against their captors or fleeing from them. The 54th had fought for African freedom on the battlefields of the Civil War. Ida B. Wells had fought for equality with her pen. Lewis H. Latimer and Meta Vaux Warrick had tried to earn equality with their work. In *Brown vs. Board of Education* Thurgood Marshall, Kenneth B. Clark, and the lawyers and social scientists, both black and white, who helped them had won for African Americans a victory that would bring them closer to full equality than they had ever been in North America. There would still be legal battles to be won, but the major struggle would be in the hearts and minds of people and "in that gap between law and custom." ❖

✳ Return to the excerpt, and in the **Response Notes,** tell why Myers would probably call "heroes" the people whose names you high-lighted. Underline the details that he gives in the excerpt.

✳ With a partner, brainstorm a list of other people you would call heroes. They can be from any time period or place. Write their names in the box below. List some qualities that make each one a hero in your opinion.

Name	Qualities

✳ Select one name and outline a short piece you could write about this person. Include in your outline the person's name, the reason you think he or she is heroic, and two or three details you could use.

_____

_____

_____

_____

_____

_____

_____

_____

Nonfiction writing
can show real people
overcoming obstacles.

Walter Dean Myers's life and beliefs are evident in his works. He does not just tell the story of his life and the people he knows, though. As an author, he crafts new stories that connect with topics that he knows well—life in Harlem, the army, teenagers, history, and so forth.

In the following excerpt, he reveals his beliefs about the importance of libraries. The 115th Street branch of the New York Public Library in Harlem had been undergoing renovation for more than three years when he wrote this opinion piece for the *New York Times*. As you read, put check marks by the details that connect with any of Myers's other writing that you have read in this unit or elsewhere.

Response Notes

from "**Hope Is an Open Book**" by Walter Dean Myers

As a child growing up in Harlem, I measured my life, and my potential, by what I saw around me. I saw first that I was black and poor. My father was a janitor, and my mother, never very healthy, cleaned apartments when she was well enough to work.

There was no single event that traumatized me, no devastating storm in my life, but slowly the life of the poor began to grind me down. A murdered uncle, an alcoholic parent, the realization that there was no way that I could afford college brought despair to my life. The promising 14-year-old I had been became the 15-year-old chronic truant who had to report to a city agency once a week for supervision.

But amid the chaos, I found a refuge. It was the New York Public Library. Not the research libraries, but the neighborhood branch where I would take out three or four books each week in a brown paper bag to avoid the comments of my friends who thought I was "acting white." When I felt least wanted by the world, the library became my bridge to self-value.

As I stumbled, on the verge of becoming a statistic in the juvenile justice system, increasingly angry at a world that I felt did not belong to me, the George Bruce branch library on West 125th Street was my home away from home. The 115th Street branch is similarly a sanctuary for residents in its neighborhood.

The library was the one place in my world that I could enter and participate in fully despite empty pockets. In the library stacks I could consider a novel by Gide or Balzac or Hemingway, and join a universe that would otherwise be denied me. There was no way I could have afforded to buy the books.

In the quiet surroundings of the library, I was safe from the hostility that many inner-city children encounter when they look to extend their lives intellectually. And, if the hostility was there when I was a child, how much more do young people face in an age in which the heroes are gangsta rappers?

I speak with thousands of young people around the country each year: youngsters in middle school, high school students and children in juvenile detention centers. I've learned that they all experience a period of transition, a time when they stop thinking of life as something that will happen to them in the future, and start examining where they are in the moment. It is at this time that their lives are most shaped by the reality of their circumstances and by their ability to escape those circumstances by reaching out for ideas that will eventually define their success in life.

For me, at that moment, the library was crucial—its doors opened onto the American dream. ✛

✳ List two ways that this text connects with other pieces by Walter Dean Myers that you have read in this unit.

1. _____

2. _____

Making connections is one way to start reflecting on the author's work. A second way is to evaluate it. When Myers works with students in schools, he introduces them to his ÉCLAIR formula to criticize material. It looks like this:

E —Emotion

C —Clarity

L —Language that sings

A —Argument

I —Imagination

R —Rhythm

He explains that by *argument* he means "that the writer wants to sway the reader toward a specific point of view. Argument has a utility that, in my view, meaning lacks." He applies this formula to all writing, including poetry.

✳ Use this chart to evaluate the writing you have read in this unit. Do you think Myers follows his own formula? In the top row, write the titles of three excerpts you read. In the other boxes, copy a short sentence or phrase that shows emotion, clarity, or other qualities of the ÉCLAIR formula. Below the chart, write your evaluation of Walter Dean Myers's writing.

Emotion			
Clarity			
Language that sings			
Argument			
Imagination			
Rhythm			

Walter Dean Myers is/is not a good writer because _____

_____

_____

_____

Reflecting on an author's life and work helps you understand the author's writing and evaluate its quality.

Assessing Your Strengths

In this *Daybook,* you have been introduced to a number of ways to become a better reader and writer, building your **repertoire of reading and writing strategies.** You have learned how to interact and connect with the stories and articles you read. You have applied multiple perspectives. You have analyzed language and craft. You have focused on one particular author. Now you are going to use all of those skills and strategies as you read new texts, explore ideas, and demonstrate your proficiency at using the skills and strategies in a piece of writing.

The texts for this unit present three different perspectives on what it means to be an outsider. You will read about ways in which people about your age were transformed by major world events that radically changed their everyday lives. First is a poem written in 1986 by a young Vietnamese refugee shortly after she came to the United States. The next two pieces are set during the era of World War II but depict widely divergent stories of young people during times of great upheaval and displacement.

INTERACTING WITH THE TEXT

Read or listen to this poem written by a young woman from Vietnam shortly after she came to the United States. Be aware of your feelings as you read or listen.

You Have to Live in Somebody Else's Country to Understand by Noy Chou

Response Notes

What is it like to be an outsider?
What is it like to sit in the class where everyone has blond hair and
you have black hair?
What is it like when the teacher says, "Whoever wasn't born here raise
        your hand."
And you are the only one.
Then, when you raise your hand, everybody looks at you and makes fun of you.
You have to live in somebody else's country to understand.
What is it like when the teacher treats you like you've been here all your life?
What is it like when the teacher speaks too fast and you are the only
one who can't understand what
he or she is saying, and you try to tell him or her to slow down.
Then when you do, everybody says, "If you don't understand, go to a
lower class or get lost."
You have to live in somebody else's country to understand.
What is it like when you are an opposite?
When you wear the clothes of your country and they think you are crazy
to wear these clothes and you think they are pretty.
You have to live in somebody else's country to understand.
What is it like when you are always a loser.
What is it like when somebody bothers you when you do nothing to them?
You tell them to stop but they tell you that they didn't do anything to you.
Then, when they keep doing it until you can't stand it any longer, you
go up to the teacher and tell him or her to tell them to stop bothering you.
They say that they didn't do anything to bother you.
Then the teacher asks the person sitting next to you.
He says, "Yes, she didn't do anything to her" and you have no witness to turn to.
So the teacher thinks you are a liar.
You have to live in somebody else's country to understand.
What is it like when you try to talk and you don't pronounce the words right?
They don't understand you.
They laugh at you but you don't know that they are laughing at you, and

you start to laugh with them.

They say, "Are you crazy, laughing at yourself? Go get lost, girl."

You have to live in somebody else's country without a language to understand.

What is it like when you walk in the street and everybody turns around

to look at you and you don't know that they are looking at you.

Then, when you find out, you want to hide your face but you don't know

where to hide because they are everywhere.

You have to live in somebody else's country to feel it. ❖

INTERACTING WITH THE TEXT AND MAKING CONNECTIONS

❋ Reread the poem, and select phrases, lines, or passages that have meaning for you. Make notes in the **Response Notes** column explaining connections you make to Noy Chou's concerns in the poem. Give examples from your own life experiences.

❋ Write about a time when you felt like an outsider or when someone made a judgment about you based on events or other issues over which you had no control.

_____

_____

_____

_____

_____

_____

_____

❋ Do you think all teenagers experience being "outsiders" in some way? Explain your opinion.

_____

_____

_____

_____

_____

_____

One primary function of literature is to help us understand the feelings and experiences of others and to see how they connect to our own lives.

Aleutian Sparrow by Karen Hesse deals with Vera, a young Aleut girl, during an event in our history that many Americans don't know about. In 1942 the Japanese bombed and occupied the islands of Kiska and Attu, located at the most northwest region of North America. Alaska was not yet a state, but was a territory of the United States. The Japanese campaign to control the North Pacific led the American government to evacuate the majority of Aleut (al-ee-UTE) residents living west of Unimak Island.

The prose poems that make up the novel *Aleutian Sparrow* are best heard read aloud in the oral tradition of the Aleuts. Listen to the first piece, "Who We Were." As you listen, use the **Response Notes** to comment, question, and make your own connections. Some of the images may seem unfamiliar to you, but try to imagine the string of islands that stretch into the Bering Sea from the mainland of Alaska. Remember, too, that an Alaskan summer has almost constant sunlight, while the winter has almost constant darkness.

BACKGROUND NOTES Recall that you read about Vera in Unit 10 of the *Daybook*. Alfred is a close childhood friend of Vera's. Vera spent much of her time in Alfred's house, with his parents and grandparents. Alfred's grandfather is describing their home on the island before they were relocated. The Aleuts refer to the mainland as "outside."

Who We Were from *Aleutian Sparrow* by Karen Hesse

Response Notes

Alfred's grandfather says, "Aleuts have been poets and artists.
We have made music.
We have guided the church and charted the sea.
Now we are trapped like the foot of a bird in the snare of war."

We were not so different, dressed in our Western clothes
      brought by the supply boats from Outside, washing
      laundry, cooking on stoves, sitting around the table
      talking.
Except that in every direction the sea surrounded us. Fierce
      winds boxed with us, like prizefighters sprung from
      four corners.
The fog carried us through the treeless hills in her fat arms,
      our faces pressed against her damp skin.
We were not so different. Except that we lived on the margin
      of a continent, content. ❖

BACKGROUND Vera, Alfred, and Pari grew up together; they were best friends. As they grew into teenagers, Pari became sicker every day. Vera slowly became aware of her feelings for Alfred.

The Terrible Beauty of Night from *Aleutian Sparrow*
by Karen Hesse

Escaping outside to the cabin steps,
      Dim lights burning up and down the row,
Alfred and I sit back-to-back and I tremble to be so near him,
      forgetting for a moment the forest and its thousand
      unnamed monsters, and Pari.
"Don't be afraid," Alfred says, sounding like an old man. I put
      my hand over my eyes so the light he makes shine
      inside me won't leak out. ✧

BACKGROUND During the time the Aleuts were living far from their homes, Vera's best friend Pari died from tuberculosis. One in every four of the evacuated Aleuts died from an illness to which they were subjected in that foreign climate and diet.

In the following poem, one of the ancient stories of the Aleuts, you learn of the origin of the book's title.

Trees from *Aleutian Sparrow* by Karen Hesse

The elders from Nikolski tell of the time before the white
      men came, when a single tree grew in the Aleutians
      and the Aleutian sparrow sang as it flew around the
      ascending trunk.
The seasoned tree proudly wore its struggle for life, and it
      alone reached up through the fog into the heavens.
The Russians chopped the tree down and built their Aleutian
      homes from its wood, and all those who touched the
      wood of that tree and lived in those homes met an
      early and mysterious death.
Here in our Southeast camp there are a thousand trees, but
      where is the Aleutian sparrow? ✧

BACKGROUND After three years, the Aleuts returned to their villages, but they found their homes trashed and burned. Little was left.

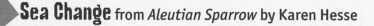

Sea Change from *Aleutian Sparrow* by Karen Hesse

After three years of promises we are back
Where the sun emerges from the galloping clouds,
     Where one moment the rain ices our hair and the next a
       rainbow arches over the volcano.

Where early grass ripples in the wind and violets lead an
       advance of wildflowers across the treeless hills.
It all comes back so quickly, the particular quality of the air
       where the Bering Sea meets the Pacific.
The Aleutian sparrow repeats over and over its welcome of
       fluid notes.
Our resentment folds down into a small package and is
       locked away under the floor of our hearts.
What other chance do we have to survive if we cannot forget?

BACKGROUND This is the last poem in the novel. The people who are still alive return home with the bodies of their friends and relatives, to bury them in their own land. In this poem you feel the spirit of the Aleuts.

Procession from *Aleutian Sparrow* by Karen Hesse

We carried
Pari and her mother home with us
And buried them under the shadow
Of Mount Newhall.

The gulls squeal overhead, and in the harbor
       A murre perches on a half-submerged wreck.
The wind whips our hair across our faces, the sun breaks
       Through to touch the grasses on the mountainside.
And as Aleuts have always done,
We find the will to begin again.

WRITING

Think about your own family's oral traditions. Are there times in your family when you gather together and the "elders" tell stories of how "it used to be"? Do you like to hear stories of when you were little, even though they might be embarrassing?

Many families today are fragmented, with members dispersed geographically. You might not have had the opportunity to hear these stories growing up. If this is the case with your family, you can imagine what stories there might have been. Many "memoirs" are filled with imagined stories.

✳ Choose one of the following two ideas for a short piece of writing. In either case, write it in the form of a prose poem.

1 Write a prose poem in the style of Karen Hesse's poems in *Aleutian Sparrow* about a tradition in your family. You might tell the story in two or three short poems.

2 Write a letter in the form of a prose poem to Vera while she is in a relocation camp. Think about what you could say to her about your own life or what questions you have about hers.

_____

_____

_____

_____

_____

_____

_____

_____

_____

_____

_____

_____

_____

_____

Basing a fictional story on a real historical event gives us insights into how that event affected the people.

The following story is in the first chapter of a **memoir** written by world-renowned concert pianist Mona Golabek. In this story Mona tells the true story of her mother's journey during World War II as she was transported from Vienna to England as part of the children's exodus, the Kindertransport. This story shows how a young girl carried with her the music instilled in her by her mother. She was a gifted pianist and became an inspiration to the other children living with her in London after being evacuated from their homes.

In this first chapter of the book, you see young Lisa Jura on a very important day, one of her last in her native city of Vienna. Use the **Response Notes** to record the images, thoughts, questions, or feelings that you have as you read this story. Remember you can cluster, write, or draw. Include notes about connections to your own experience. Put a star by the scenes that are most vivid for you.

from The Children of Willesden Lane by Mona Golabek and Lee Cohen

Response Notes

Lisa Jura took her appearance very seriously. She stood in front of the mirror for an eternity, arranging her dark red hair so that it peeked stylishly from under the wool hat she had just bought in the hand-me-down store. The hat needed the perfect tilt . . . just so. She had seen the models do it in the fashion magazines.

She was determined to look more sophisticated than her fourteen years. She was going to her piano lesson and there was nothing more important. Finally turning from the mirror, she smiled at the image of a saucy young girl.

After opening the front door quietly, so as not to disturb her family, she walked down the hallway of the crowded tenement and emerged from the solemn gray building, stepping onto the sidewalk of Franzensbrückestrasse in the heart of the Jewish section of the city.

As she had done every Sunday since her tenth birthday, Lisa boarded the lumbering streetcar and crossed Vienna, heading for Professor Isseles's studio.

She loved the ride.

The images rushed by her window—the glorious Ferris wheel of the Prater amusement park and the blue and serene Danube—eerily accompanied by the distant rhythm of an oompah band. To go across the city was to enter another century—the era of grand palaces and stately ballrooms. Street upon street of marble and granite, of pillar and pediment. The spire of St. Stephen's Cathedral danced by. Her father called it *"Der Alte Steffe"*—"Old Stevie." Lisa

thought it a silly name; it was much more grand than that, rising to the heavens like a castle in a fairy tale.

As the streetcar descended the broad avenue and passed Symphony Hall, Lisa closed her eyes, just as she had many times before, and imagined herself sitting perfectly still in front of the grand piano on the stage of the great auditorium. A hush fell over the audience. The keys shimmered in front of her, ebony against ivory. She could hear the opening of Grieg's heroic piano concerto: the soft roll of the tympani building until the moment of her entrance. She straightened her back into the elegant posture her mother had taught her, and when the tension was almost unbearable she took a breath and began to play.

She could sense the excitement of the audience and feel their hearts beat in time with hers. The exhilaration of hearing the music inside her was so extreme that the bumps of the ride and the noise of the street no longer disturbed her.

When she finally opened her eyes, the car was passing the Ringstrasse, the majestic tree-lined boulevard where the Grand Court Opera House stood. She looked out the window in awe and waited for the driver to call her stop.

This was the Vienna of Mozart, Beethoven, Schubert, Mahler, and Strauss, the greatest composers of all time. Lisa's mother had filled her head with their stories, and she had made a secret vow to live up to their legacy. She could hear their music in the marble of the buildings and the stones of the streets. They were here. They were listening.

In a booming voice, the driver called out her stop. But today his words were strange and different. In place of the familiar "Mahler-Strasse" she was expecting, he called another name: "Meistersinger-Strasse." Lisa's heart stopped momentarily.

She climbed down into the great plaza. All the street signs had been changed; the Nazis did not approve of such a grand avenue being named after a Jew. She felt her fury grow but tried to contain herself. Getting upset would only interfere with her music. She forced herself to think about the lesson ahead, knowing that once she was at the piano, the world outside would disappear.

Although it was early, the café-lined streets bustled with energy. The gentle sounds of the "Blue Danube" waltz, mixing with raucous Dixieland jazz, returned the smile to Lisa's face. The aroma of warm, fresh *apfelstrudel,* thick with sliced apples and cinnamon, made her long for a taste of her mother's recipe—surely the best in all of Vienna.

Inside the cafés, well-dressed young men and women sipped their coffee, deep in animated conversation. Lisa imagined them all to be composers, artists, and poets passionately defending their latest works. She yearned to join them, to wear fine clothes and speak of Beethoven and Mozart—to be a part of that intoxicating café society. One day, when she made her musical debut, these streets, these cafés, would be hers.

When Lisa reached her destination, she stopped short. A German soldier, tall and emotionless, stood in the doorway of the old stone building that housed Professor Isseles's music studio. The sun glinted harshly off the black rifle he held against his gray uniform.

She had been coming to the professor's studio for nearly four years, but this was the first time anyone had been standing guard. She shouldn't have been surprised, though; Nazi guards were becoming an increasingly menacing sight on the streets of Vienna.

He asked coldly, "What business do you have here?"

"I have a piano lesson," she replied, trying not to be frightened by the soldier's commanding presence or by the firearm on his shoulder.

"The professor will be waiting," she continued in a loud, clear voice, the force of her words belying her true state of mind. The soldier looked up to the second-floor window. A figure stared down, then motioned that it was all right for the girl to come up. Lowering his weapon, the soldier moved away from the door and grudgingly allowed Lisa to pass.

"Come in, Miss Jura," Professor Isseles said, greeting Lisa with his customary warm handshake. The stoop-shouldered, white-haired gentleman ushered her in past a chipped bust of Beethoven and a sideboard covered with stacks of yellow sheet music. She breathed in the aroma of the professor's pipe tobacco. These sights and scents had become a friendly greeting—a signal that for the next hour, she could turn away from all else and be a part of the music she loved.

The professor's stately Blüthner piano stood in the middle of the studio. It was richly polished, with ornately carved legs and a scroll-patterned music stand. On the wall hung her teacher's prized possession—a photograph of Franz Liszt as an old man, surrounded by several students, including the professor's teacher. He boasted that his teachings were a direct line from the master himself, and there was a worn mark on the photograph where he had so often placed his finger.

As usual, there was little small talk. Lisa put the score of Beethoven's Piano Concerto no. 1 in C on the music stand and sat on the worn piano bench. She adjusted its height to fit her small stature.

"So, Miss Jura, was it difficult?" asked the professor.

"It was much too easy," she teased.

"Then I expect nothing less than perfection," he responded, smiling.

Lisa began to play the tender C-major opening theme. The professor sat forward in his chair and followed her progress with his copy of the score. When the simple theme erupted into cascades of descending arpeggios, she peered out of the corner of her eye to judge his reaction.

She hoped to catch him smiling. After all, she had learned the complicated first movement in only a week and had often heard him say that she was his best student.

But the professor continued listening with a stern concentration. When he had this expression, she imagined it was his sadness at not being able to play the piano anymore. Arthritis had stiffened his fingers, making it impossible to demonstrate the correct way of playing. What a cruel trick of fate to deny a pianist the ability to perform, she thought. She could not imagine a day when she would not be able to play.

To illustrate his lessons, Professor Isseles would play recordings for her on his gramophone. He was in awe of Horowitz's playing of Rachmaninoff, but it was the lyricism of Myra Hess performing Beethoven that he most appreciated.

"Listen to the tone of her legato," the professor would say with a sigh.

Lisa listened and listened and listened.

For most of the hour Lisa played uninterrupted, as the old man sat in silence, occasionally bringing his hand down to emphasize an accent in the music. Finally, he put down his music and just listened. She looked over and saw a distressed expression on his face. Was she playing that badly?

At the end of the piece, the professor made no comment. Lisa went on to her customary scales and waited anxiously for her assignment. The professor focused on scraping the bowl of his pipe into the ashtray.

"May I do the adagio for next week?" she asked nervously. She loved the second movement and yearned to show him her improving legato.

He looked at her for a long moment, then finally spoke, looking uncomfortable and ashamed: "I am sorry, Miss Jura. But I am required to tell you that I cannot continue to teach you."

Lisa was stunned and unable to move. The professor walked to his window and opened the curtain. He stared at the people in the street. "There is a new ordinance," he said slowly. "It is now a crime to teach a Jewish child." He continued mumbling under his breath, then added in despair, "Can you imagine!"

Lisa felt tears rising.

"I am not a brave man," he said softly. "I am so sorry."

He came over to the piano, lifted up her slender young hands, and held them in his grip. "You have a remarkable gift, Lisa, never forget that."

Through her tears, she watched the professor pick up a thin gold chain that lay on top of the piano. It held a tiny charm in the shape of a piano.

"It is not much, but perhaps it will help you to remember the music we shared here," he said softly, fastening the gold chain around her neck with trembling fingers.

She stared through her tears at the stacks of music, the picture of Liszt on the wall, and tried to memorize every detail. She was afraid she might never see them again. Gathering her composure, she thanked the professor and collected her things, then turned and fled. ❖

RESPONDING TO THE STORY

✳ Answer these questions.

■ What kind of person is Lisa Jura and how do you know?

_____

_____

■ What do you think of Professor Isseles? What gives you that impression?

_____

_____

■ What are some of the clues that the Nazis are beginning to take over the city?

_____

_____

■ What are some of the things that are as important to you as music is to Lisa Jura?

_____

_____

A *memoir* is a story based on real people and their lives. The reader gets to know well the subject of a memoir.

The three texts in this unit each deal with a young displaced person. In the poem, "You Have to Live in Somebody Else's Country to Understand," the young refugee has not yet found a way to deal with the feelings of being an outsider. In *Aleutian Sparrow,* Vera copes with the displacement, carrying both the sadness and the hope of the Aleuts as she returns home. The young musician in *The Children of Willesden Lane* carries with her the power of music instilled by her mother.

WRITING PROMPTS

✳ Choose one of the following prompts and write two to three pages in response. Use the next page to plan your writing, but use your own paper for the rest of this assignment.

1 **Narrative** Write a narrative about a time when you had to leave your school or community and felt like an outsider in the new place. Be sure to use specific, sensory details as well as figurative language to allow the reader to see, hear, and feel the actions and emotions of the characters in your narrative. Use quotations in your paper from one or more of the texts you read in this unit.

2 **Prose Poems** Write a series of prose poems about a time when you felt like an outsider in a new place. Be sure to use specific, sensory details as well as figurative language to allow the reader to see, hear, and feel the actions and emotions of the characters in your narrative. Refer in your paper to one or more of the texts you read in this unit.

3 **Reflection** Write about the teenager as an outsider in our society. What are the things that make so many teenagers feel like outsiders? What can the school or community do about this situation? Use specific examples in your paper. Refer in your paper to one or more of the texts you read in this unit.

SELECT A TOPIC

✳ After you select a prompt, make a list of possible ideas on which to focus. Then, circle the idea that you will use.

GATHER DETAILS

✳ Now that you have a topic, you need to decide what to write. Make a list or create a graphic organizer (a web or a chart) in which to collect your details. Include information from your own life to support the prompt. For example, if you're writing about an event, include details about where and when it took place, who was there, what you were thinking, and so forth. Also make a note of details and quotations in the selections that support your writing.

✳ Once you have settled on your topic and gathered supporting details, you can begin to draft your writing on a separate piece of paper.

Using references to your reading in your writing shows that you understand the important ideas.

SHARING YOUR FIRST DRAFT

As with any craft, an important part of writing is looking to see how it can be improved. In writing, this is called **revision** because you *see* (vision) it *again* (re). Use the list below to evaluate your writing. You might want to meet with a partner and review each other's papers, as well.

- Does my paper respond directly to one of the three prompts?

- Are my ideas about the concept of an outsider clear?

- Are my ideas organized in an appropriate way?

- Does the beginning grab the reader's attention so that he or she wants to read more? If not, how could it be improved?

- Is the end of the paper satisfying? Does it sound "finished"? If not, what could I do to make a better ending?

- Have I chosen my words carefully—specific nouns and vivid verbs?

- Does the language in my paper "show" the reader what is happening, as opposed to just "telling"? In other words, have I used concrete details and sensory language?

- Do my sentences flow so that the paper can be read aloud easily?

- Are the beginnings and lengths of my sentences varied?

- Have I checked for spelling, punctuation, and capitalization errors?

✻ Read your paper aloud to a partner or members of a small group. When each person finishes reading, the other members should tell the reader what they liked about the paper. As you listen, refer to the items in the list to help the reader strengthen the paper. As your group talks about your paper, make notes so that when you revise it, you will remember what they suggested.

MAKING A FINAL COPY

✻ Using the suggestions of your group, make all the revisions you think will improve your paper. Then make a clean copy of your final draft. Remember to give it a title.

A FINAL REFLECTION

As you worked through this *Daybook,* you have had many opportunities to learn and practice skills and strategies to become a better reader and writer.

✳ In this final reflection, consider how much you have improved as a reader and writer during your work with the *Daybook.* Write a few paragraphs reflecting on how you have improved and what you can do to become an even stronger reader and writer than you are now.

_____

_____

_____

_____

_____

_____

_____

_____

_____

_____

_____

_____

_____

_____

_____

_____

_____

_____

Reflection is an important part of learning how to identify and improve on your strengths as a reader and writer.

GREAT SOURCE. COPYING IS PROHIBITED.

Becoming An Active Reader

Reading can entertain, inform, and reward. Reading also requires some hard work on the part of the reader. The sections that follow will help you get the most out of your reading.

The **reading process** section will guide you through reading a text. It will help you think about how to prepare to read (before reading), what to think about as you read (during reading), and how to get the most out of your reading by reflecting on it (after reading).

The **reading actively** section will show you how to interact with a text in order to get the most meaning out of it. It will show you how to engage with a text by using your brain and your pen—both at the same time!

The Reading Process has three parts: **Before Reading, During Reading,** and **After Reading.**

1. BEFORE READING

❊ Preview the Material

Look over the selection before you read. Does the selection look like a short story or other work of fiction? If so, look at the title, introduction, and illustrations. Does the selection look like nonfiction? If so, look for headings, boldfaced words, photos, and captions. Also, ask yourself how the information is organized. Is the author comparing or contrasting information about the topic? Is the information presented in a sequence using signal words like first, second, third, and finally? Understanding how an author has organized information will help you to recognize key points as you read.

❊ Make Predictions

When you make predictions, you actively connect with the words on the page. Think about what you already know about the subject or the images. Then, think of yourself as a text detective, putting together what you know with new details in the text. Predict what you think will happen, why an event caused something to happen, or what might come next in a series of events.

❊ Set a Purpose

Begin by reviewing what you already know about the topic or situation in the text. Then, think about what you want to find out.

QUESTIONS TO ASK YOURSELF BEFORE READING

■ Before I read this material, what do I think it is going to be about?

■ After looking over the selection, what do I already know about this subject?

■ What should I be thinking about as I read?

2. DURING READING

✳ Engage with the Text

As your eyes look at the words, your brain should be working to make connections between the words and what you already know. Have you had an experience similar to that of one of the characters in a story you are reading? Do you know someone like the character? Have you read another book about the topic? You will also want to connect what you read to the predictions you made before reading. *Confirm, revise, predict again* is a cycle that continues until you finish reading the material. All of these questions will go on inside your head. Sometimes, though, it helps to think out loud or write.

✳ Monitor Your Understanding

As you read, stop from time to time and ask yourself, "Do I understand what I just read?" If the text doesn't make sense, there are several steps that you can take.

- Go back and reread the text carefully.
- Read on to see if more information helps you understand.
- Pull together the author's ideas in a summary.
- Retell, or say in your own words, the events that have happened.
- Picture in your mind what the author described.
- Look for context clues or word-structure clues to help you figure out hard words.

This takes some practice. Remember, to be a successful reader, you must be an active reader. Make an effort to check your understanding every so often when you read a new selection.

QUESTIONS TO ASK YOURSELF WHILE YOU ARE READING

- What important details am I finding?
- Which of these ideas seem to be the most important?
- Does this information fit with anything I already know?
- What do I see in my mind as I read this material?
- Do I understand the information in the charts or tables? Does it help me to understand what I am reading?

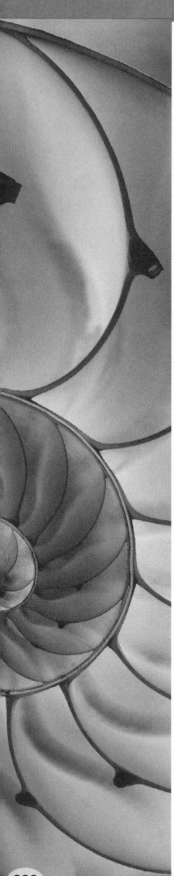

3. AFTER READING

✳ Summarize

Reread to locate the most important ideas in the story or essay.

✳ Respond and Reflect

Talk with a partner about what you have read. What did you learn from the text? Were your predictions confirmed? What questions do you still have? Talking about reading helps you to better understand what you have read.

✳ Ask Questions

Try asking yourself questions that begin like this:

Can I compare or contrast . . . evaluate . . . connect . . . examine . . . analyze . . . relate . . .

✳ Engage with the Text

Good readers engage with a text all the time, even when they have finished reading. When you tie events in your life or something else you have read to what you are currently reading or have read, you become more involved with your reading. In the process, you are learning more about your values, relationships in your family, and issues in the world around you.

QUESTIONS TO ASK YOURSELF AFTER READING

- What was this article about?
- What was the author trying to tell me?
- Have I learned something that made me change the way I think about this topic?
- Are there parts of this material that I really want to remember?

Make the effort to stay involved with your reading by reading actively. Your mind should be busy reading the text, making connections, making predictions, and asking questions. Your hand should be busy, too. Keep track of what you are thinking by "reading with your pen." **Write** your reactions to the text or connections that you can make. **Circle** words you don't understand. **Draw** a sketch of a scene. **Underline** or **highlight** an important idea. You may have your own way of reading actively. You may develop a style that works better for you, but here are six common ways of reading actively.

MARK OR HIGHLIGHT The most common way of noting important parts of a text is to write on a sticky note and put it on the page. Or, if you can, mark important parts of a text by highlighting them with a marker, pen, or pencil. You can also use highlighting tape. The highlighted parts should provide a good review of the text.

ASK QUESTIONS Asking questions is a way of engaging the author in conversation. Readers who ask a lot of questions think about the text more and understand it better. "Why is the writer talking about this?" "Is this really true?" "What does that mean?"

REACT AND CONNECT When you read, listen to the author and to yourself. Think about what you are reading and relate it to your own life. Compare and contrast what the text says to what you know.

PREDICT Readers who are involved with the text constantly wonder how things will turn out. They think about what might happen. They check their thoughts against the text and make adjustments. Sometimes the author surprises them! Making predictions helps you stay interested in what you are reading.

VISUALIZE Making pictures in your mind can help you "see"what you are thinking and help you remember. A chart, a sketch, a diagram— any of these can help you "see." Sometimes your picture doesn't match what you think the author is telling you. This is a signal to reread to check your understanding of the text.

CLARIFY As you read, you need to be sure that you understand what is going on in the text. Take time to pull together what you have learned. Try writing notes to clarify your understanding. Another way of checking to see that you understand is to tell someone about what you have read.

GLOSSARY

abandoned left alone

abash to make uncomfortable or ill at ease

adagio a slow tempo

adolescence the period of life between childhood and adulthood

allusion an indirect reference

American Indian Native American

anguish emotional pain

annunciation usually refers to the biblical announcement to Mary that she was going to bear Jesus

arc a curved path

argument persuasive language consisting of a main idea supported by details and reasons

arpeggio a technique of playing the notes of a chord one after another

artillery large, heavy weapons operated by more than one person

art of language style and structure

assent to agree

atomic age the period after World War II, when people realized that mass destruction could be caused by nuclear bombs

autopilot an airplane's system for flying itself so a pilot does not have to be at the controls all of the time

B-29 a military plane that carried bombs

backwash cultural influence

banshee a female spirit in Gaelic folklore whose wailing foretold a death

barracks a large, plain building used for temporary housing

barrage an attack coming from many different directions at once

barrow a cart for moving heavy things

Beard, James (1903–1985) an influential cooking teacher

bedroll a mat that is placed on the floor and used for sleeping

beheld looked at and studied

betimes quickly

bistro a small restaurant

Boanerges a person who talks very loudly

bog moist; spongy ground

Boricua a person who is Puerto Rican in blood and soul

boycott to avoid purchasing or using a product because you object to conditions under which it is grown or made

bracero a Mexican laborer permitted to enter the United States and work for a limited period of time

breechcloth a cloth worn over the lower body

bulbous rounded, bulb-shaped

calligraphers people who create stylized, artistic lettering

caribeña Spanish term for a girl or woman from the Caribbean

chaired lifted up on a chair or on the shoulders of other athletes

chicken pox a disease that leaves crater-like marks on the skin if not treated carefully

Chugoku name of Hiroshima's newspaper

collective bargaining negotiation between organized workers and their employer to determine wages, hours, and working conditions

commune with get messages from

conceived envisioned; thought of

concerto a musical work that focuses on a soloist or a group of soloists

conjure to bring about as if by magic

connecting to the story being emotionally involved with the story

consecrate make holy

continental food food of European cultures, such as French, German, or Italian

contraband smuggled goods

crooned sung in a soft, gentle manner

corridos Mexican ballads or folk songs

counterpane an embroidered quilt; a bedspread

credible believable or trustworthy

croon to sing with a low, gentle tone

cuddles holds someone close

default to fail to pay debts

deliberating considering carefully

demur to disagree

detract reduce in size or impact

dewy covered with dew

diaspora the scattering of a people

Dickinson, Emily reclusive, prolific American poet of the mid-1800s

discerning able to see clear differences

disciplinarian someone who corrects others' behavior with rules and punishments

disfiguring something that leaves a mark on the skin or changes the shape of a feature

disheartening discouraging

docile obedient

Douglass, Frederick African American orator and abolitionist

dreary dull; boring; gloomy

dregs solid parts left behind in a mostly liquid food or drink

Du Bois W.E.B. Du Bois; writer, educator, and civil rights leader in the first half of the 20th century

dumfounded surprised and confused (usually spelled dumbfounded)

Emperor the ruler of an empire; in this case, the Japanese empire

employee discharges people who have been relieved of their war duties

etching a fine-lined image printed from a cut metal plate

evaluating deciding on the value of something

evidence facts that support an argument

exalted held up in honor

examining multiple viewpoints reading different points of view of a story in order to look at a moment or event from more than one angle

exotic charming because of unfamiliarity

extremity a state of extreme need

eyewitness a person who sees an event first-hand

fleet fast; rapid

flung thrown

foodie's mecca a place where food lovers find many restaurants and food shops

forager someone who "hunts" for food that grows wild

foreman a person who serves as the leader of a work crew

furrowed wrinkled

gingko a species of tree that originated in China and that has fan-shaped leaves

grainy not clear; appearing to be made out of small (grain-like) particles

haft the handle of a tool

Hail Mary a Roman Catholic prayer to Mary, who was the mother of Jesus

hallow make holy

hew carve

hidebound made narrow-minded

historical fiction fiction set in the past, in a time of important historical events

hobbled tied the front legs of a horse together to keep it from wandering

Homer ancient Greek poet credited with the creating of *The Iliad* and *The Odyssey*

host large group of people

hullabaloo a loud noise

humanities school subjects of English, history, and social studies

icon someone who receives a lot of attention for what they symbolize

image mental picture created by a reader as he or she reads

impolitic socially unwise

impulsively without thinking

in vain for no purpose

inadequacy lack of ability

infer to make an inference

inferences reasonable guesses you make by putting together something you have read with something you already know

infused flavored with something, such as garlic (usually said of a liquid)

innocuous harmless

intangible not "touchable"; conceptual, as opposed to physical

integrated open to all people

interacting with the text "carrying on a conversation" with a text; a strategy for effective reading that involves circling, underlining, and writing notes

interposition placing obstacles between people

intuitive inborn

jíbara Spanish term for a female peasant

lap to be an entire circuit ahead of a competitor on a race around a track; to lick

lauding praising

laurel branches of a laurel tree traditionally used to honor athletes

legato a smooth tempo

Lenox Avenue a street in Harlem in New York City

lintel top of a door or window

Little Boy the code name for the atomic bomb dropped over Hiroshima

livelong entire and tedious

living inside the story feeling so connected to a story that you are completely drawn in

loathsome much-hated

localize to keep from spreading

lolling reclining in a relaxed way

lyricism a light, bright musical style

magenta a bright purplish red

magnesium a metal that sizzles when burned

making connections a reading strategy that involves comparing what you are reading to something you already know

manacles metal shackles for hands or feet, usually attached to chains

massacre mass murder

Mayflower the ship on which the pilgrims came to America

medicine man Native American healing priest

memoir a writer's written reflections on his or her earlier life

mestiza Spanish term for a girl or woman of mixed blood; usually referring to those of both European and Native American ancestry

metacognitive awareness the process of thinking about what's going on in your mind as you do something

metamorphosizes transforms, changes into a different form

metaphor a technique of figurative language in which one thing is described in terms of something else

mija Spanish term of endearment; literally, "my daughter"

mingle to mix or blend together

miserly extremely small and insufficient

modeling a poem using the structure of a poem as a foundation for a new poem

Moses a Hebrew leader who led his people away from enslavement

mushroom cloud the kind of cloud that is caused by a nuclear explosion, usually appearing the shape of a mushroom

N.A.A.C.P. National Association for the Advancement of Colored People; an organization formed in support of civil rights for people of color

Nazi abbreviated name of the political party headed by Adolf Hitler

nonfiction factual writing

nullification rejection of federal law by a state government

nymph an imaginary, fairy-like creature

obligation something you have to do

odious hated or disgusting

off-notes unintended aromas that arise when a flavor or scent reacts with something

omnipotent all-powerful

organic grown without chemicals

ostracize to exclude someone

Oy gevalt! Yiddish exclamation of surprise or alarm

pallor a pale or faint color

parchment writing surface similar to paper, but made from goat or sheep skin

pare to trim away an edge

patron person who supports an artist or a cause; sponsor

personal narrative a short prose piece in which a writer expresses personal thoughts and makes connections

personnel employees of a company

persuasion an attempt to convince others to feel the same way you do

pigeon-holed strictly categorized; from the old-fashioned desk with small compartments called pigeon-holes because they resemble the compartments that homing and racing pigeons sleep in

perspective the point of view or angle from which you see a subject

plaintively sadly

plot how the characters and events in a story are connected

pogrom organized massacre of a minority group

Pole a Polish person

pragmatism practicality

prefecture government officials of the region

prodigious enormous; huge

prohibitions orders to stop actions

promissory note an agreement to pay back a loan

prosecutor lawyer whose job it is to prove the guilt of the accused

protectorate a country or region controlled or protected by another

psyche human spirit

pulp publication containing mostly sensational subject matter

puritanical related to the Puritans; extremely strict in matters of morals

purpose an author's intent in writing

pustules small skin sores

raggy slang for ragtime, an early form of jazz characterized by uneven rhythms

ration food given by the government during war or other emergencies

recluse a person who stays separate from the rest of the world

Reich Germany or the German government during one of the three reichs; in this case, during the Third Reich, 1933–1945

relegate assign to an unimportant place

repertoire of reading and writing strategies a collection of learned abilities needed by an effective reader and writer

repetition the repeating of a word or phrase to emphasize a point

restaurateur restaurant owner

reverently with awe and respect

revision looking at a draft again in order to find ways to improve it

revolution a big change in the way people think or act

Robinson, Jackie first African American to play major league baseball

root ball the tangled roots of a plant

rouge red coloring for cheeks

rout a retreat or flight from defeat

saintly completely good, or unable to be criticized

sanitarium a place for healing; from the root *sanitas,* meaning "good health"

savage wild, fierce

scenario a setting and brief sequence of events

score twenty

scrounge to beg or forage

scuffling struggling at close quarters

scullery a room for washing dishes

segregated having separate laws or facilities for separate groups of people

sharecropper a tenant farmer who gives a share of the crops to the landlord as rent for the land

shtetl a small Jewish town formerly found in Eastern Europe

simile a technique of figurative language in which the characteristics of one thing are described in terms of something else using the word *like* or *as*

sledgehammer a long, heavy hammer used to break up things

solemnly seriously

soprano in music, a voice that can sing the highest notes

sore severe

sorest most urgent

sound-bite culture group of people who only pay attention to small bits of information and do not take the time to understand longer discussions

squalor dirtiness and poor condition due to poverty and neglect

stance the way someone is standing

starkest most extreme

stopped plugged up

straightway immediately

strategy a carefully designed plan of action for reaching a goal

structure the way a piece of writing is put together, as shown by the arrangement of its words, sentences, paragraphs, chapters, and so on

stud a wooden frame inside a wall

style a writer's unique way of writing, as shown by the decisions the writer typically makes as to sentence length, description, figurative language, and tone

subtle barely noticeable

suffocation in this context, denseness and airlessness

supercilious proud; arrogant

supporting evidence facts, statistics, examples, observations, quotations, and experts' opinions that support an argument

sustainable not permanently removing resources from the environment

sustenance something that people need to live, such as food

symbol image or object that represents other things

synagogue a Jewish place of worship

syncopated a musical device common in jazz consisting of a shift of accent to a normally weak beat

Taína female member of an ancient Caribbean people

tallow fat from cows that is used to make candles, soap, and food

tangible something "touchable"; an object

tatami a straw mat that is laid on the floor

theme the main topic or message that is explored through the characters and plot of a story

thesis statement the part of a persuasive piece of writing that expresses the author's main idea

threescore sixty (score = 20)

tipi cone-shaped house made of poles, animal skins, and tree bark

tone the author's attitude toward his or her subject, as shown by word choice and sentence structure

treacherous sneaky; likely to betray

trowel a small garden tool with a flat blade for digging

tuberculosis a contagious lung disease with symptoms that include fever, weight loss, chest pain, and coughing up sputum

Tubman, Harriet African American "Angel of Mercy" in the mid-19th to early 20th centuries; best known for leading slaves to freedom along a route called the Underground Railroad

tympani two or more kettledrums

unborn not yet born

uncanny so amazing as to be almost frightening

unconstitutional not in agreement with the U.S. Constitution

vegetarian someone who eats no meat

venue place

veranda a porch or balcony that has a roof

visualizing a reading strategy in which a reader makes pictures in his or her mind of a text

voice the narration style of an author

war bonnet a special head covering with feathers and other decorations

willow a species of tree that has thin, narrow leaves

wiry thin

Wittgenstein Ludwig Josef Johan Wittgenstein, an Austrian-born British philosopher of the early 20th century

Wrangell Institute a large boarding school for Native American children

ACKNOWLEDGMENTS

10 "Alabama Earth", "Luck" by Langston Hughes. Used by permission of Random House, Inc.

13 "Aunt Sue's Stories" by Langston Hughes. Used by permission of Random House, Inc.

16 From *The Return of Simple* by Langston Hughes. Used by permission of Random House, Inc.

19 "The Weary Blues" by Langston Hughes. Used by permission of Random House, Inc.

22 From *I Wonder as I Wander* by Langston Hughes. Used by permission of Random House, Inc.

26, 29 Copyright © 1996 by Russell Freedman. All rights reserved. Reprinted from *The Life and Death of Crazy Horse* by permission of Holiday House, Inc.

31 Brief text as submitted from *The Autobiography of Eleanor Roosevelt* by Eleanor Roosevelt. Copyright 1937, 1949, © 1958, 1961 by Eleanor Roosevelt. Copyright © 1958 by Curtis Publishing Company. Reprinted by permission of HarperCollins Publishers.

34, 37 Wall Street Journal.

40, 43, 46 "The Circuit", from *The Circuit: Stories from the Life of a Migrant Child* by Francisco Jimenez. Copyright © 1997 by Francisco Jimenez. Reprinted by permission of Houghton Mifflin Company. All rights reserved.

49 Excerpt from "In the Strawberry Fields" by Eric Schlosser, *The Atlantic Monthly,* Vol 276, Iss 5, Nov 1995. Used by permission.

51 From "A Street Name That Hits Home" by Tara Malone. Reprinted by permission of Daily Herald.

54, 57 From *Hiroshima* by John Hersey. Used by permission of Random House, Inc.

60 Excerpt from "Summer Flower" by Tamiki Hara, from "The Crazy Iris". Used by permission of Grove/Atlantic Inc.

63 From *Shockwave: Countdow to Hiroshima* by Steven Walker. Used by permission of HarperCollins Publishers.

66 From *Hiroshima, A Novella* by Laurence Yep. Copyright © 1995 by Laurence Yep. Reprinted by permission of Scholastic, Inc.

70 From *A Sky Full of Poems* by Eve Merriam. Copyright © 1964, 1970, 1973, 1986 by Eve Merriam. Reprinted by permission of Marian Reiner.

74 "anyone lived in a pretty how town". Copyright © 1940, 1968, 1991 by the Trustees for the E.E. Cummings Trust, from *Complete Poems: 1904-1962* by E.E. Cummings, edited by George J. Firnage. Used by permission of Liveright Publishing Corporation.

77 Mark Turpin, "Sledgehammer Song" from *Hammer*. Copyright © 2003 by Mark Turpin. Reprinted with the permission of Sarabande Books, Inc., www.sarabandebooks.org.

79 From *The Pearl* by John Steinbeck, copyright 1945 by John Steinbeck, © renewed 1973 by Elaine Steinbeck, Thom Steinbeck and John Steinbeck IV. Used by permission of Viking Penguin, a division of Penguin Group (USA).

79 "Skin", an excerpt from "The Story of My Body", from *The Latin Deli: Prose and Poetry* by Judith Ortiz Cofer. Copyright © 1993 by Judith Ortiz Cofer. Reprinted by permission of the publisher, The University of Georgia Press.

86, 89, 91, 98 Reprinted by permission of the publishers and the Trustees of Amherst College from *The Poems of Emily Dickinson,* Thomas H. Johnson, ed., Cambridge, Mass.: The Belknap Press of Harvard University Press, Copyright © 1951, 1955, 1979, 1983 by the President and Fellows of Harvard College.

98 "To an Athlete Dying Young" from Authorised Edition of *The Collected Poems of A.E. Housman*. Copyright 1924, 1965 by Henry Holt and Company. Reprinted by permission of Henry Holt and Company, LLC.

105 From *The Frog Prince Continued* by John Scieszka, © 1991 by John Scieszka. Used by permission of Viking Penguin, A Division of Penguin Young Readers Group, A Member of Penguin Group (USA) Inc., 345 Hudson Street, New York, NY 10014. All rights reserved.

110 "Annunciation" used by permission of Adrianne Marcus.

116, 119 Excerpts from "Food Product Design", from *Fast Food Nation* by Eric Schlosser. Copyright © 2001 by Eric Schlosser. Reprinted by permission of Houghton Mifflin Company. All rights reserved.

122 Copyright © 2004 Peggy Orenstein. Reprinted by permission.

125 Reprinted by permission of *Publicaffairs*, a member of Perseus Books.

128 Excerpt from *Ruth Reichl: A Taste for Life*. Used by permission of the American Booksellers Association.

135, 137 From *Maus I: A Survivor's Tale/My Father Bleeds History* by Art Spiegelman, copyright © 1973, 1980, 1981, 1982, 1984, 1985, 1986 by Art

Spiegelman. Used by permission of Pantheon Books, a division of Random House, Inc.

142 From *Memories of Anne Frank: Reflections of A Childhood Friend* by Alison Leslie Gold. Published by Scholastic Press/Scholastic, Inc. Copyright © 1997. Reprinted by permission.

146, 149, 152 Excerpts from *When My Name Was Keoko* by Linda Sue Park. Copyright © 2002 by Linda Sue Park. Reprinted by permission of Clarion Books, an imprint of Houghton Mifflin. All rights reserved.

155 Reprinted with the permission of Margaret K. McElderry Books, an imprint of Simon & Schuster Children's Publishing Division from *Aleutian Sparrow* by Karen Hesse. Text copyright © 2003 Karen Hesse.

158 "Sunday, October 6, 1991", "Monday, March 30, 1992", "Sunday, April 5, 1992", "Monday, June 29, 1992" from *Zlata's Diary* by Zlata Filipovic, copyright © 1994 Editions Robert Laffont/Fixot. Used by permission of Viking Penguin, a division of Penguin Group (USA) Inc.

162 Excerpt is used with the permission of the Special Collections, University of California, Riverside.

168 Reprinted by arrangement with the Estate of Martin Luther King, Jr., c/o Writers House as agent for the proprietor New York, NY. Copyright 1963 Martin Luther King, Jr., copyright renewed 1991 Coretta Scott King.

178 Text copyright © 1988 by Paul Fleischman. Used by permission of HarperCollins Publishers.

182 "On Turning Ten" is from *The Art of Drowning*, by Billy Collins, © 1995. Reprinted by permission of the University of Pittsburgh Press.

186 "Life Doesn't Frighten Me", copyright © 1978 by Maya Angelou, from *And Still I Rise* by Maya Angelou. Used by permission of Random House, Inc.

186 "Alone", copyright © 1975 by Maya Angelou, from *Oh Pray My Wings Are Gonna Fit Me Well* by Maya Angelou. Used by permission of Random House, Inc.

190 "Ending Poem" from "Getting Home Alive" by Rosario Morales and Aurora Levins Morales, © 1986, Firebrand Books, Ann Arbor, MI.

194 From *Bad Boy: A Memoir* by Walter Dean Myers. Used by permission of HarperCollins Childrens Books.

197 From *The Glory Field* by Walter Dean Myers. Copyright © 1994 by Walter Dean Myers. Reprinted by permission of Scholastic, Inc.

200 From *Monster* by Walter Dean Myers. Used by permission of HarperCollins Childrens Books.

203 From *Now Is Your Time* by Walter Dean Myers. Used by permission of HarperCollins Childrens Books.

206 © 2005, The New York Times. Reprinted by permission.

210 Published in 1986 by the Anti-Defamation League for the "A World of Difference" project.

212 Reprinted with the permission of Margaret K. McElderry Books, an imprint of Simon & Schuster Children's Publishing Division from *Aleutian Sparrow* by Karen Hesse. Text copyright © 2003 Karen Hesse.

216 From *The Children of Willesden Lane* by Mona Golabeck and Lee Cohen. Copyright © 2002 by Mona Golabeck and Lee Cohen. By permission of Warner Books, Inc.

ILLUSTRATIONS

137: © Great Source; **142** *m:* © Laszlo Kubinyi. Reprinted by permission of Houghton Mifflin Company. All rights reserved. All additional art created by AARTPACK, Inc.

PHOTOGRAPHY

Photo Research AARTPACK, Inc.

cover, 1: © Royalty-Free/Corbis; **3–7:** © Brand X Pictures.

Unit 1 9: © Photodisc/Getty; **10:** © Corbis; **11:** © Royalty-Free/Corbis; **12:** © Royalty-Free/Corbis; **13:** © Royalty-Free/Corbis; **14:** © Royalty-Free/Corbis; **15:** © Royalty-Free/Corbis; **16:** © Royalty-Free/Corbis; **18:** © Photodisc Green/Getty; **19:** © Digital Vision/Getty; **20:** © Getty Images; **21:** © Digital Vision/Getty; **22:** © Royalty-Free/Corbis; **23:** © Corbis; **24:** © Royalty-Free/Corbis.

Unit 2 25: © Stone/Getty; **26:** © Royalty-Free/Corbis; **27:** © Royalty-Free/Corbis; **28:** © Comstock Images; **29:** © Photodisc/InMagine; **30:** © Photodisc/InMagine; **31:** © Getty Images; **32:** © Bettmann/Corbis; **33:** © Royalty-Free/Corbis; **34:** © Flip Schulke/Corbis; **35:** © John Arthur Stokes; **36:** © Bettmann/Corbis; **37:** © Royalty-Free/Corbis; **38:** © Royalty-Free/Corbis.

Unit 3 39: © Steve Starr/Corbis; **40:** © Royalty-Free/Corbis; **42:** © Image Source/Getty; **43:** © Photodisc Green/Getty; **44:** © Photodisc Green/Getty; **45:** © Glowimages/Getty; **46:** © Stone/Getty; **47:** © Photodisc Green/Getty; **48:** © Ryan McVay/Getty Images; **49:** © Image Source/Getty; **51t:** © Najlah Feanny/Corbis; **51b:** © PhotoAlto/Getty; **52:** © Glowimages/Getty.

Unit 4 53: © The Image Bank/Getty; **54:** © Ablestock/InMagine; **55:** © Ablestock/InMagine; **56:** © Murat Taner/

zefa/Corbis; **57t:** © John Van Hasselt/Corbis Sygma; **57b:** © Royalty-Free/Corbis; **58:** © Royalty-Free/Corbis; **59:** © Murat Taner/zefa/Corbis; **60:** © Robert Essel NYC/Corbis; **61:** © Corbis; **62:** © Robert Essel NYC/Corbis; **63:** © Nathan Benn/Corbis; **64:** © Bettmann/Corbis; **65:** © John Van Hasselt/Corbis Sygma; **66:** © John Van Hasselt/Corbis Sygma; **67:** © Brand X Pictures; **68:** © Brand X Pictures.

Unit 5 69: © Royalty-Free/Corbis; **70:** © 1997 PhotoDisc, Inc.; **71t:** © Richard Hamilton Smith/Corbis; **71b:** © Takashi Sato/Sebun Photo/Getty; **72:** © 1997 PhotoDisc, Inc.; **73:** © Richard Hamilton Smith/Corbis; **74:** © Image Source/Getty; **75:** © Image Source/Getty; **76:** © Brand X Pictures; **77t:** © Comstock Images; **77br:** © Photodisc Green/Getty; **77bmr:** © Photodisc Green/Getty; **77bml:** © Photodisc Green/Getty; **77bl:** © Photodisc Green/Getty; **78:** © Comstock Images; **79:** © Digital Vision/Getty; **80:** © Digital Vision/Getty; **81:** © Royalty-Free/Corbis; **82:** © Royalty-Free/Corbis; **83:** © MedioImages/Getty; **84:** © MedioImages/Getty.

Unit 6 85: © Bettmann/Corbis; **86t:** © 1993 PhotoDisc, Inc.; **86b:** © 1993 PhotoDisc, Inc.; **87t:** © 1993 PhotoDisc, Inc.; **87b:** © 1993 PhotoDisc, Inc.; **88:** © Comstock Images; **89t:** © 1993 PhotoDisc, Inc.; **89b:** © 1993 PhotoDisc, Inc.; **90:** © Royalty-Free/Corbis; **91t:** © Royalty-Free/Corbis; **91b:** © 1993 PhotoDisc, Inc.; **92:** © Natphotos/Getty Images; **93:** © Photodisc/InMagine; **94:** © Photodisc/InMagine; **95:** © Indexstock/InMagine; **96:** © Indexstock/InMagine; **97:** © Comstock Images; **98:** © Ingram/InMagine; **99:** © Ingram/InMagine; **100:** © Photonica/Getty.

Unit 7 101: © David Aubrey/Corbis; **102:** © Jim Zuckerman/Corbis; **103:** © Photodisc Red/Getty; **104:** © Photonica/Getty; **105:** © Photodisc Red/Getty; **106:** © Photodisc Green/Getty; **107:** © Photodisc Green/Getty; **108t:** © Scott Gries/Getty; **108b:** © Michele Constantini/Getty; **109:** © 1996 PhotoDisc; **110:** © Stone/Getty; **111:** © 1996 PhotoDisc; **112:** © Photonica/Getty; **113r:** © Blend Images/Getty; **113b:** © Royalty-Free/Corbis; **114:** © Blend Images/Getty.

Unit 8 115: © Stone/Getty; **116:** © Matthew Mcvay/Corbis; **117:** © Comstock, Inc.; **118:** © Royalty-Free/Corbis; **119:** © Tetraimages/InMagine; **120:** © Comstock, Inc.; **121:** © Ross Durant/Jupiter Images; **122:** © Photodisc Red/Getty; **123t:** © Comstock, Inc.; **123m:** © Comstock, Inc.; **123b:** © Comstock, Inc.; **124:** © Royalty-Free/Corbis; **125:** © Roger Ressmeyer/Corbis; **127:** © Royalty-Free/Corbis; **128:** © Foodcollection/InMagine; **129:** © Envision/Corbis; **130:** © MedioImages/Getty.

Unit 9 131: © Medioimages/InMagine; **132t:** © 2005 Comstock Images; **132b:** © Gianni Giansanti/Sygma/Corbis; **134:** © Michael St. Maur Sheil/Corbis; **135:** © Michael St. Maur Sheil/Corbis; **137:** © Corbis; **139:** © Bettmann/Corbis; **140:** © Royalty-Free/Corbis; **141:** © 2005 Comstock Images; **142:** © Reuters/Corbis; **143:** © Hulton Archive/Getty; **144:** © Royalty-Free/Corbis.

Unit 10 145: © Art Wolfe/Getty; **146:** © Robert Essel NYC/Corbis; **147:** © Michael S. Yamashita/Corbis; **148:** © Royalty-Free/Corbis; **149:** © Jason Hosking/zefa/Corbis; **151r:** © Jason Hosking/zefa/Corbis; **151b:** © Royalty-Free/Corbis; **152:** © Tongro/InMagine; **153:** © Royalty-Free/Corbis; **154:** © Tongro/InMagine; **155:** © Kevin Schafer/Corbis; **156:** © 1996 PhotoDisc, Inc.; **157:** © 1996 PhotoDisc, Inc.; **158:** © Reuters/Corbis; **160l:** © Reuters/Corbis; **160b:** © BrandXPictures/InMagine.

Unit 11 161: © Paul Edmondson/Corbis; **162:** © Swift/Vanuga Images/Corbis; **164:** © Patricia Canova Tipton/Jupiter Images; **165:** © Patricia Canova Tipton/Jupiter Images; **166:** © Corbis; **167:** © Royalty-Free/Corbis; **168:** © Flip Schulke/Corbis; **169:** © Flip Schulke/Corbis; **170:** © Hulton-Deutsch Collection/Corbis; **171:** © Hulton-Deutsch Collection/Corbis; **172:** © Flip Schulke/Corbis; **173:** © Bettmann/Corbis; **174:** © Digital Vision/Getty; **175r:** © Time & Life Pictures/Getty; **175m:** © Royalty-Free/Corbis; **176:** © Echos/Jupiter Images.

Unit 12 177: © Sven Hagolani/zefa/Corbis; **178:** © 2005 Comstock Images; **179:** © Photodisc Green/Getty; **180t:** © Photonica/Getty; **180b:** © Photodisc Green/Getty; **181:** © Photonica/Getty; **182:** © Stone/Getty; **183:** © Photodisc Green/Getty; **184:** © Stone/Getty; **185:** © Royalty-Free/Corbis; **186:** © Royalty-Free/Corbis; **187:** © Adnan Abidi/Reuters/Corbis; **188:** © Brand X Pictures; **189:** © Brand X Pictures; **190:** © 1999 PhotoDisc, Inc.; **191:** © Stone/Getty; **192:** © James Sparshatt/Corbis.

Unit 13 193: © Royalty-Free/Corbis; **194:** © Royalty-Free/Corbis; **195:** © Getty Images; **196:** © Royalty-Free/Corbis; **197:** © The Image Bank/Getty; **198:** © 1997 PhotoDisc, Inc.; **199:** © 1997 PhotoDisc, Inc.; **200:** © Royalty-Free/Corbis; **201:** © Photodisc Green/Getty; **202:** © Photodisc Green/Getty; **203:** © Bettmann/Corbis; **204:** © Ablestock/InMagine; **205:** © Photographer's Choice/Getty; **206:** © Rudy Sulgan/Corbis; **207:** © Royalty-Free/Corbis; **208:** © Bettmann/Corbis.

Unit 14 209: © Royalty-Free/Corbis; **210:** © Andrew Holbrooke/Corbis; **211:** © Simon Marcus/Corbis; **212:** © Macduff Everton/Corbis; **213:** © Altrendo/Getty; **214t:** © Shaen Adey/Gallo Images/Getty Images; **214b:** © Tim Thompson/Corbis; **215:** © Shaen Adey/Gallo Images/Getty Images; **216:** © Ingolf Pompe/Getty; **217:** © Hulton-Deutsch Collection/Corbis; **219:** © Stone/Getty; **220:** © Christine Schneider/zefa/Corbis; **221:** © Photodisc/InMagine; **222:** © Photodisc/InMagine; **223:** © Royalty-Free/Corbis; **224:** © Time & Life Pictures/Getty.

Becoming an Active Reader 225: © Rayman/Getty; **226-228:** © 1997 PhotoDisc, Inc.; **229:** © Birgid Allig/zefa/Corbis.